THE HARLOW CAR
BOOK OF
Herb Gardening

THE HARLOW CAR
BOOK OF
Herb Gardening

Philip Swindells

DAVID & CHARLES
Newton Abbot · London · North Pomfret (Vt)

(FRONTISPIECE) The herb garden at Harlow Car

British Library Cataloguing in Publication Data

Swindells, Philip
  The Harlow Car book of herb gardening.
  1. Herb gardening
  I. Title
  635'.7   SB351.H5

  ISBN 0-7153-8829-0

Typeset by Typesetters (Birmingham) Ltd,
Smethwick, West Midlands.
Colour origination by Columbia, Singapore.
Printed and bound in West Germany by
Mohndruck GmbH
for David & Charles Publishers plc
Brunel House   Newton Abbot   Devon

Published in the United States of America
by David & Charles Inc
North Pomfret   Vermont 05053   USA

Contents

Introduction

Over the past few years at Harlow Car Gardens – home of the Northern Horticultural Society – the cultivation of herbs has come into its own. From a modest border of culinary herbs in 1980, development has continued so that now the Gardens boast a specially constructed herb garden as well as a collection of herbs, dyeing and perfumery plants. These are also accommodated in other parts of the Gardens.

As an educational and research organisation, the Northern Horticultural Society is not only interested in gathering together herb plants, but more particularly in observing and recording their behaviour in a cold northern climate. Most herbs prefer a warm sunny situation on free draining land, so the cool air and cold uncompromising clay soil of the area are a good test of a plant's ability to perform satisfactorily in Britain. The information gleaned is then invaluable to gardeners all over the country.

Being in the heart of Yorkshire and the old textile industry, plants that were used for dyeing are also of great interest to us, and a collection of these has become well established, together with many old-fashioned herb plants whose cultivation has declined with changing fashions.

Apart from being an excellent source of information for the enthusiastic grower, the herb plant collections at Harlow Car are a source of plant material for conservation; seeds gathered from many herbs are distributed annually to other institutions and enthusiastic amateur gardeners.

I have included in this book all plants that are, or have been, commonly used for culinary, medicinal or perfumery purposes, regardless of their botanical characteristics, thus bringing in the shrubby plants such as witch hazel and elder. The herbal plants themselves are an enormous pot-pourri of the plant kingdom, and I hope you will come to cultivate and enjoy them as much as I have.

Philip Swindells
CURATOR, HARLOW CAR GARDENS

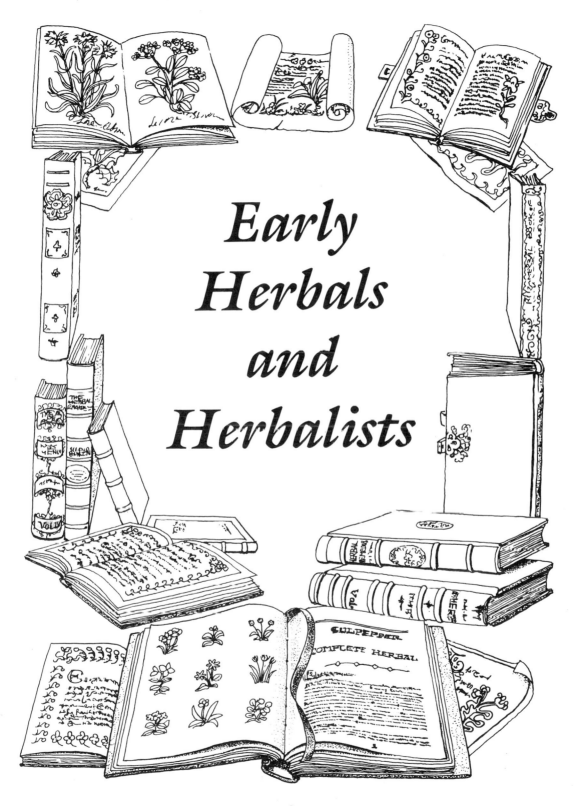

Early Herbals and Herbalists

*H*ERBS have been used by man for many thousands of years. The Greeks were amongst the first people to document the use of herbs. Early Greek doctors were known as aesclepiadiae, followers of Aesculapius, the god of medicine, and amongst these was Hippocrates of Cos (469–399 BC) the 'Father of Medicine', undoubtedly the most famous of all. He is credited with assembling one of the earliest lists of herbs, comprising some four hundred different kinds. However, most scholars believe that, as with his sixty or more other scientific works, it was merely his name that was appended to the findings of the medical school of the Greek Island of Cos collectively known as the *Corpus Hippocraticum* (Hippocratic Collection).

As time progressed, more extensive records of herb usage were provided by Dioscorides (AD 40–90) who compiled a list of six hundred different plants and their uses. This was one of the most important herbals to be written, playing a major part in herbalism until the publication of *The Herbal* (1597) by John Gerard in the sixteenth century. It is said that Gerard based his famous book upon an indirect translation of the work of Dioscorides. The herbal of Galen (AD 131–201), physician to Marcus Aurelius, was another important complementary work on herbal botany. Together with the writings of Pliny the Elder (AD 23–79), who expounded upon most flowers and herbs that were known at that time in his monumental *Natural History*, these works form the basis of our early knowledge of herbs and herbalism.

Although interest in herbs continued in the East they had little prominence in the West until the Swiss scientist von Hohenheim, (better known as Paracelsus, 1493–1541), and his contemporary the Italian physician della Porta, working independently, came up with an idea which was eventually to be known as the Doctrine of Signatures. This theory suggested that the Almighty had marked

Purists seek to recreate the atmosphere of the monastic era when herb growing was the prerogative of the learned few. Even in a small garden this feeling of peace and mystery can be achieved by the careful selection and planting of traditional herbs

various plants in significant ways to indicate to man which disorders they would cure. This was widely accepted and actively promoted in a book entitled *The Art of Simpling* (1656) by William Coles. Occasionally enthusiasts for this theory accidentally did come up with the correct plant for alleviating a malady, but this was more by luck than sound knowledge. Most recommendations were totally ineffective, such as red-flowered plants being used for disorders of the blood, or spotted-leaved subjects being a cure for pimples. Later disciples of the theory, trying to restore its credibility, pointed out that plants of the family *Cruciferae* do not include any poisonous species, therefore the arrangement of their four-petalled flowers in the shape of a cross must be a sign that these plants are safe and edible!

In Britain as elsewhere in Europe, monks and priests also left us records of early herb culture, some of the oldest documents being written by Alexander Neckham, Abbot of Cirencester, and Bishop Grosseteste of Lincoln. Both compiled lists of herbs cultivated in the early monastery gardens, significant amongst these being parsley, sage, savory, rue, mint, fennel, southernwood, and hyssop. However, the most revered writings of the time came from William Turner (1510–1568), Dean of Wells, who was doctor and gardener as well as priest and who later became known as the Father of English Botany.

If there were to be nominations for the Father of English Herbalism, then Nicholas Culpeper (1616–1654) would head the list. The son of a clergyman, he studied to become a doctor, eventually establishing a practice as both a medical man and an astrologer. He wrote a number of medical and botanical books, the most significant being *The English Physitian Enlarged*. This describes in detail the drying of herbs and their preparation into pills, ointments and potions, giving us a detailed look at the early use of herbs in medicine.

Herbs have been cultivated for medicinal purposes for a few thousand years but those of culinary, fragrant or decorative value only were not recorded to any great extent until the eighteenth and nineteenth centuries. Amongst the books written around that period were those on pot-pourri by Mrs C. W. Earle (1836–1925). Mrs Earle wrote a number of classics in which herbs figure prominently. *Pot-Pourri From A Surrey Garden* (1897), *More Pot-Pourri* (1899) and *A Third Pot-Pourri* were the three most successful titles. Her only serious contender in this field has been Eleanor Sinclair Rohde (1881–1950), an excellent gardener and author of many gardening books, including *The Old English Herbals* (1922), *The Scented Garden* (1931) and *Herbs and Herb Gardening* (1936). Today there are a number of knowledgeable and enthusiastic herb growers and nurserymen who are recording their efforts in the cultivation and uses of herbs. Over the years the image and uses of herb plants have varied widely, but man's interest in them has remained constant.

Herbs and their Modern Uses

*H*ERBS have many merits, but the one that usually attracts the gardener is their culinary value. From earliest days until Victorian and Edwardian times herb gardening was the commonest form of gardening practised by the 'common' man. Only the large estates could afford to use plants purely for decorative purposes. Herb gardening and herb usage declined during the early twentieth century but has in recent years regained its great popularity.

Herbs are more than merely fashionable today. Modern gardeners are much better informed about culinary herbs, and many herb gardens are regularly cropped for leaves, roots and seeds. In fact, this kind of herb patch is best accommodated in a sunny corner of the vegetable garden. Most plants used as culinary herbs benefit from constant trimming, pinching and cutting. An unused herb garden soon becomes overgrown and untidy.

HERBS AS FLAVOURINGS

While a number of herbs, like chervil, can be made into soups themselves the majority are used as flavourings in a wide variety of other dishes, such as soups, casseroles, pasta and raw in salads. Many foods are enhanced by the addition of one or more accompanying herbs.

Anise
  bread, cakes
Balm
  chicken, meat, vegetables
Basil
  eggs, meat, tomato
Bergamot
  pork, salads
Caraway
  cabbage, carrot, cheese, pork, salads
Chervil
  eggs, cheese, chicken, fish, lentils
Chives
  eggs, cheese, salads, tomato
Comfrey
  salads
Coriander
  bread, curry, pickles, sauces
Costmary
  peas, stuffings
Cumin
  curry, meat
Curry Plant
  eggs, fish, meat, sauces
Dill
  eggs, fish, pickles, vegetables
Fennel
  fish, salads, sauces, soup
Garlic
  chicken, fish, meat, mushrooms, pasta, potato, tomato, vegetables
Horseradish
  beef
Hyssop
  pork, salads, soup
Lemon Balm
  chicken, fish, stewed fruit
Lemon Thyme
  chicken, fish, fruit

Lemon Verbena
  fruit, salads
Lovage
  chicken, meat, salads, sauces, soups, stews
Marjoram
  fish, meat, onion, peas, potato, tomato
Mint
  carrot, lamb, peas, potato
Mugwort
  goose, pork
Parsley
  chicken, fish, potato, soup, tomato
Pot Marigold
  omelettes, salads
Rosemary
  chicken, lamb
Sage
  duck, onion, pork
Salad Burnet
  salads, sauces
Sorrel
  salads
Summer Savory
  beans, fish
Sweet Cicely
  fruit, salads
Tarragon
  chicken, fish, mushrooms, tomato, vegetables
Thyme
  chicken, fish, meat, onion, tomato, vegetables
Winter Savory
  beans

COOKING WITH HERBS

Many parts of herb plants are suitable for use in cooking, such as leaves, seeds, roots and, occasionally, flowers. Most are best used in their fresh form, but this is not always practical, especially during the winter months. Drying is perfectly satisfactory if carefully executed with plant material that is in peak condition. Culinary herbs are used to add flavour to cooked meat and fish dishes, as raw garnishings for salad, and as an important constituent of soups and stews. Various sauces to accompany dishes originate from herb plants, while a number figure as an important ingredient in drinks. Their usefulness and diversity in the kitchen is endless.

SCENTED HERBS FOR POT-POURRI

Most herb plants are rich in oils, indeed it is these that give the plants their aromatic qualities and form the basis for many perfumes. The successful production of perfume from the home garden is very difficult, but an easy way to enjoy the sweet fragrances of herbs, is to make your own pot-pourri – a mixture of dried petals and foliage from the most fragrant plants placed in a decorative container where it can fill a room with scent.

Petals must be dried at a lower temperature than leaves and should be selected when each blossom is at its peak. Unfortunately the choice of strongly scented blossoms is somewhat limited, but a little dried and grated orange or lemon peel can be incorporated to strengthen the aroma. It is essential to add a fixative such as orris root, which can be obtained from a beauty shop or herbalist.

An attractive scented corner could include sage, angelica, lemon balm, cotton lavender, lavender, chives and pinks. The shorter subjects disguise the unsightly lower foliage of their taller neighbours

HERBAL TEAS

It was originally the medicinal properties of herbs that attracted man, and many are still used as remedies today. Others are valuable for their soothing, calming or refreshing properties, and herbal 'teas' are now becoming increasingly popular as replacements for traditional stimulants such as tea and coffee.

It is quite simple to make your own teas from homegrown herbs, using fresh or dried leaves, seeds, roots or sometimes the flowers, as in chamomile tea. You need a pot or jug, made of anything other than aluminium, with a tight-fitting lid. Add 2 generous handfuls of fresh leaves (2 tsp dried leaves), pour on 500ml (1pt) boiling water, replace the lid and leave to infuse for 5 minutes or to taste. Treat seeds, roots and flowers in the same way, where appropriate (see table below).

HERB	PART USED	BENEFIT OR REMEDY
Angelica	Roots, seeds, leaves and stems	For colds, coughs, flatulence and rheumatism.
Anise	Seeds	For colds, catarrh and asthma.
Balm	Leaves (picked before flowering)	For influenza and catarrh. A most refreshing lemon-flavoured summer drink mixed with honey. Also mixes with Indian tea.
Bergamot	Leaves	A refreshing summer drink. Mixes with Indian tea successfully.
Borage	Leaves and flowers	Fever and kidney problems. A pleasant summer drink.
Caraway	Seeds	Used in an infusion to relieve indigestion.
Chamomile	Flowers	Sedative, relieves headaches and chest complaints.
Coriander	Seed and fresh leaves	Coriander water is used to relieve flatulence and colic.
Costmary	Fresh leaves	Anti-spasmodic and astringent.
Dandelion	Roots, flowers and leaves	Relieves biliousness.
Dill	Young leaves and seeds	The seeds used in an infusion relieve indigestion.
Elderflower	Flowers	Laxative. Also relieves cold symptoms.
Hyssop	Fresh green tops	Relieves chest troubles such as asthma and is used for muscular rheumatism.
Mint (spearmint and peppermint)	Leaves	Aids digestion and also used for nausea and flatulence.
Parsley	Leaves, stems and roots	Formerly used for kidney disorders, jaundice and dropsy.
Rosemary	Young tops, leaves and flowers	A relief for headaches, colic, colds and nervous depression.
Rue	Leaves	A remedy for colic and 'female' disorders.
Sage	Leaves	Used for head colds, sore throats, gum disorders and nervous headaches.
Sweet Cicely	Root	Revives the appetite. Also useful for coughs.

Pot-pourri is best accommodated in a decorative container of glass or similar transparent material with a tight-fitting lid so that the rustic brown, gold and green hues of the dried foliage can be enjoyed with the pinks and purples of the flower petals. When not in use, it is a wise precaution to put on a tight-fitting lid and place the pot-pourri in a dark cupboard to help reduce the fading of the contents and retain the perfume.

Rosemary, lavender, bay, chamomile and thyme all have leaves that respond well to the needs of the pot-pourri maker, while roses, pinks, and carnations provide scented petals that can be successfully dried. To add a little lighter colour, dry some elder blossoms, or delicate creamy mullein flowers. Some favourites of mine for the pot-pourri are: mints (especially eau-de-cologne mint), lemon balm, catmint, tarragon and cotton lavender.

Pot-pourri can be made from a mixture of leaves and petals dried and placed in a small container. Most plants that are rich in aromatic oils can be successfully dried

HERB VINEGARS

Herb vinegars are marvellous for flavouring salads, dressings and sauces – and they are very simple to make. Pick the leaves on a dry day just before the plant flowers, and strip the leaves from the stalks.

Tarragon vinegar is particularly useful and versatile, especially for tomato, chicken and fish salads; and tartare, bearnaise and hollandaise sauces.

To make your own tarragon vinegar, allow 225g (8oz) leaves to 2 litres (3½pt) white wine vinegar. Bruise the leaves, place in a bottle or jar, fill with vinegar and cover tightly. Leave to steep in a cool, dry place (in the dark if using clear glass bottles) for 6–8 weeks. Strain through muslin into a new bottle and add a fresh sprig of tarragon.

Basil, sage, thyme, marjoram, salad burnet, lemon balm, dill, fennel, and mint vinegars can all be made in the same way. Red wine or cider vinegar can be used for variation.

How we use pot-pourri today is very reminiscent of the way in which our forebears would use strewing herbs on the floor. In Elizabethan times, and before, herbs were used extensively for scenting the often unpleasant air of dwelling houses. Full-length stems of herbs like tansy and woodruff were cut just before flowering, and spread on the floor. As people walked upon the herbs their sweet fragrance would be released to perfume the air. The foliage would usually remain in the home until dry and crisp, by which time its fragrance had dissipated, except for some herbs like tansy which retain their pungency for many weeks. In addition to the traditional herbal plants, other unassociated subjects were also grown for strewing, one of the most popular being the sweet flag, *Acorus calamus*, which has a fragrance like fresh tangerines. This is a strong-growing aquatic plant with richly fragrant iris-like foliage, allegedly introduced to Britain by monks for the sole purpose of strewing. Nowadays it is used by gardeners as an attractive plant for poolside planting.

Sweet flag was traditionally used for strewing, but today it makes an attractive poolside plant

HERBS FOR COSMETICS

The use of herbs in cosmetics has a long history, with most popular varieties being used at some time. Many are of doubtful value, but some have persisted for centuries and are well established and widely accepted. English lavender in its many fragrant guises is world renowned; here it seems to find the optimum conditions for the production of the volatile oil so valuable for perfumes, soaps and other toiletries. Elderflower water used to be almost as popular, although it has now declined in importance. It is still used by those seeking a safe skin tonic, and is reputed to tone down freckles and skin blemishes – it even makes a refreshing after-shave lotion.

Elderflower water was often used as an addition to bath water, as were lovage and rosemary foliage (the latter being boiled first). Apart from its usefulness for the skin, rosemary is also credited with being able to stimulate hair growth and has long been an ingredient in herbal shampoos. Hyssop has been attributed with cleansing properties since biblical times, though it is best known, even today, for its use in perfumes.

DYE PLANTS

Early man extracted dyes from plants with which to stain his body. Today vegetable dyes are very much in vogue and it is from those we popularly call herb plants that many of these dyes are extracted. I have included in this book a number of plants which were primarily cultivated for their dyes, although they are now used exclusively for decoration.

While it is not the purpose of this book to investigate all the intricacies of dyeing with plants, a glimpse behind the scenes might encourage the inquisitive to have a go themselves. However, it is not something that should be pursued by the impatient, for the gathering of plant material and the preparation of the fabric to be dyed is time-consuming. It should also be mentioned that

> **ELDERFLOWER WATER**
>
> This beauty treatment was once widely used and is still said to be of great benefit as a complexion lotion. Fill a jar with elder flowers stripped from their stems and cover with boiling water. Once slightly cooled add 20g (¾oz) of rectified spirits per litre (2pt). Keep covered and strain when cool. (Obtain rectified spirits from a herbalist or chemist).

Native and naturalised plants that have been used for dyeing: (*from top*) tansy (yellow or orange); cow parsley (yellow); woad (blue); yellow flag (yellow); parsley (green); dandelion (magenta) and lady's bedstraw (orange-red)

BASIC DYEING WITH HERBS

Much vegetable matter can be used to obtain a dye and the natural colours, whilst being difficult to repeat once obtained have a softness, uniqueness and charm that cannot be competed with by synthetic dyes. The herbs shown with colour indications (page 27) and those herbs referred to (page 30) will give guidance to those readers who would like to try their hand at dyeing with herbs.

Of all the fibres that are available to experiment on with plant dyes, it is wool that is the easiest with which to succeed and for our instructions we will assume the dyeing of 1lb (0.4kg) of wool.

The person who undertakes fabric dyeing regularly will, to be efficient, require a regular work area, a number of utensils, a heat source for boiling and simmering, and a supply of preferably soft water. The experimentalist can make do but never use cooking utensils as some dyes and mordants leave a poisonous residue.

There are three stages to dyeing – washing, mordanting, dyeing and drying. The washing is to clean out the natural oils, grease and dirt from the wool. The mordanting is to assist in fixing the dye chemically. The dyeing most obviously is to introduce the colour to the fibre.

Washing
You will need:
1lb (0.4kg) wool (either raw fleece or in the yarn)
1 large enamel pan
soft water
soap (in a perfect world the use of a lather prepared from common soapwort would be ideal, never use detergents or hard water)
heat source

Mordanting
You will need:
4 galls (18 litres) soft water
a large enamel pan
old spoon
1lb (0.4kg) washed wool
3oz (85g) potassium aluminium sulphate (alum powder)
1oz (28g) cream of tartar
heat source
glass rod or clean stick
rubber gloves
old cloth

Dyeing and drying
You will need:
The herb dye material
knife
chopping board
muslin bag
*a vessel for the dye bath
4 galls (18 litres) soft water
1lb (0.4kg) of mordanted wool
rubber gloves
a little ammonia

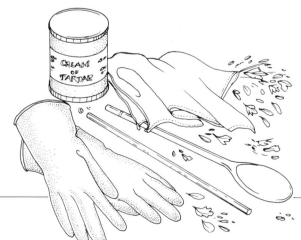

Method:

Warm the soapy water in the pan before adding the wool. Then put the pan on the heat and allow it to simmer for up to an hour making sure that the wool stays below the level of the water and the water below boiling point. Let the water cool before removing the wool. Then rinse the wool in water of approximately the same temperature until the soap is cleared away.

Method:

Mix the alum powder and cream of tartar in a cupful of water. Heat the water in the pan and add the cupful of mixture as the water starts to warm. Add your 1lb of washed wool and move it about in the mixture with the rod or stick, raising the temperature to boiling point, but not taking it beyond. This should be done gradually, allowing about an hour from adding the mixture until attaining boiling point. Simmer for another hour before removing the wool and gently squeezing out surplus liquid. After squeezing place the wool on the cloth and allow it to dry slowly in a dark place.

Alternative mordant:

Using bichromate of potash is similar but only use ½oz (14g) of the mordant with 1oz (28g) cream of tartar. This should be dissolved in a cupful of boiling water before being added to 4 galls (18 litres) water. After the requisite period in boiling water (as for alum) the wool should be rinsed and placed directly into the dye bath. As this mordant is light sensitive the wool should be completely submerged and placed in a dark place.

Method:

Chop up the dye plant material, place in a muslin bag and suspend in the bath of water overnight. Boil until the colour of the liquid seems satisfactory. (The finished wool will be lighter). If the colour appears insufficiently dense the addition of a drop of ammonia will help to release more into the water. Let the water cool, add the wool, raise the temperature and allow to simmer until you believe you have reached the desired colour. Remove the wool and rinse in water of the approximate temperature of the dyebath. The last rinse can be lukewarm. Dry outside if possible away from direct light and heat.

Never use a vessel with a rim on the bottom over a gas flame

despite the subtlety of colours that can be obtained using vegetable dyes, many are not as fast as their synthetic counterparts.

The diversity of plants that have been used for dyeing is nearly as great as those that were used medicinally. This includes many of our native and naturalised plants like cow parsley *Anthriscus sylvestris* (yellow); yellow flag *Iris pseudacorus* (yellow); tansy *Tanacetum vulgare* (yellow or orange); woad *Isatis tinctoria* (blue); dandelion *Taraxacum officinale* (magenta); lady's bedstraw *Galium verum* (orange-red); and parsley *Petroselinum crispum* (green). Not all the colours are yielded by the foliage or flowers, some give dyes from fruits or, more commonly, from their roots. These colours vary in intensity and their ability to 'take' to the material depends upon the material and the mordant used. Mordants are chemicals which are used to treat material before the application of the dye. They are usually regarded as essential for the successful application of vegetable dyes, except those obtained from lichens. Mordants not only help the dye to stay fast, but can alter the colour that is yielded. Anyone who is seriously interested in dyeing should seek a good book on the subject where the use of mordants is fully explained. However, the enthusiast who just wants to experiment a little can still derive a tremendous amount of enjoyment from the use of dye plants and raw wool. Providing that wool has not been bleached, most vegetable dyes will yield a satisfactory result. Of course, many gardeners will not grow herbs for any of the reasons that I have mentioned. They love them just for their warm fragrance, attractive foliage and colourful blossom. As most herbs come from similar climates and have common soil requirements, they are easily grown together. An added bonus is their ability to attract wild life. Bees, butterflies and moths love sweetly scented herbs and provide movement and sound in the fragrant air.

A fragrant corner for butterflies and bees. Even unlikely species such as rosebay willowherb can be incorporated to great effect, provided that their fading flower spikes are removed to prevent seeding. Also included here are (*from left*) soapwort, yarrow, thyme, marjoram, and peppermint

The Herb Garden at Harlow Car

This herb garden developed from a modest border of culinary herbs in 1980 to the specially constructed herb garden for which the provisional planting plan is shown overleaf

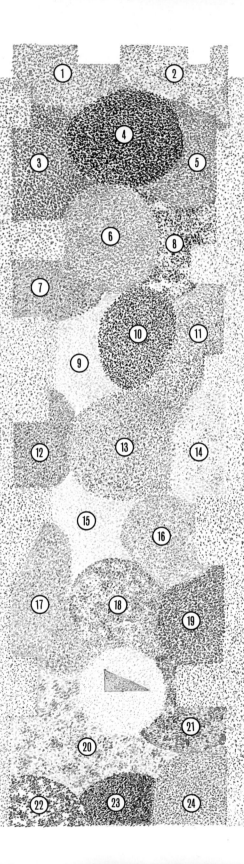

1 *Lavandula* 'Munstead'

2 *Santolina neapolitana*

3 *Mentha spicata*

4 *Rosmarinus officinalis*

5 *Satureja montana*

6 *Symphytum officinale*

7 *Asperula odorata*

8 *Anthemis nobilis*

9 *Origanum vulgare* 'Aureum'

10 *Levistichum officinale*

11 *Chenopodium bonus-henricus*

12 *Salvia officinalis* 'Purpurescens'

13 *Rumex acetosa*

14 *Salvia officinalis* 'Iceterina'

15 *Melissa officinalis* 'All Gold'

16 *Santolina neapolitana*

17 *Lavandula* 'Munstead'

18 *Anthemis tinctoria*

19 *Mentha cordifolia rubra rariparia*

20 *Melissa officinalis* 'Aurea'

21 *Thymus vulgaris*

22 *Mentha gentilis* 'Variegata'

23 *Laurus nobilis*

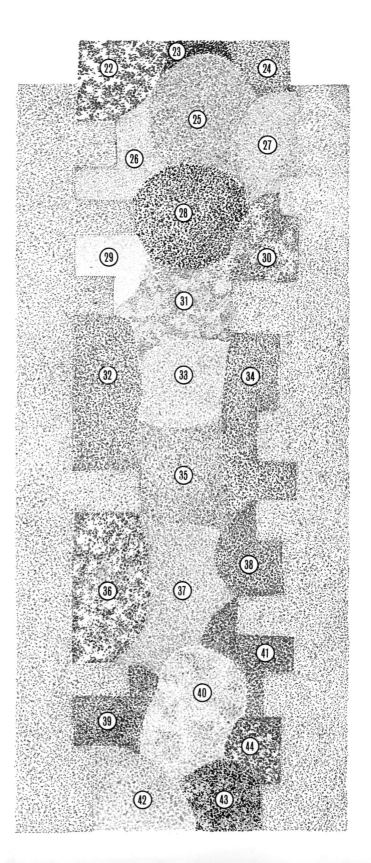

HERBS IN THE HARLOW CAR HERB GARDEN

Some of the herbs in the Harlow Car Herb Garden are fancy varieties of common culinary herbs. These will be found with other culinary herbs as they can be used for flavouring, although their main role is decorative.

Culinary Herbs

Allium cepa var.

A.schoenoprasum

Artemisia dracunculus

Chenopodium bonus-henricus

Cochleria armoracia

Foeniculum vulgare (bronze form)

Hyssopus aristatus

Laurus nobilis

Ligusticum officinale

Marrubium vulgare

Melissa officinalis

M.o.'All Gold'

M.o.'Aurea'

M.o.'Variegata'

Mentha piperata

M.rotundifolia 'Variegata'

M.spicata

Origanum marjorana

O.(vulgare) 'Aureum'

Poterium sanguisorba

Rosmarinus officinalis

Rumex acetosa

Salvia officinalis 'Albiflora'

S.o.'Icterina'

S.o.'Purpurescens'

S.o.'Tricolor'

Satureia montana

Thymus citriodorus

T.vulgaris

T.v.'Aureus'

Medicinal Herbs

Anthemis nobilis

Ruta graveolens

Dyeing Herbs

Anthemis tinctoria

Genista tinctoria

Perfumery Herbs

Asperula odorata

Lavandula 'Munstead'

Mentha citrata

Fragrant Decorative Herbs

Mentha cordifolia rubra rariparia

M.gentilis 'Variegata'

Santolina neapolitana

Herbs
for
All Gardens

HERBS FOR ALL GARDENS

*T*HERE are no strict traditions in herb gardening
for man has nurtured these plants for centuries.
However, in monasteries herb gardens developed
roughly along similar lines and this regimented
style of herb growing has now been accepted as
traditional, although a number of other styles may
also be of similar vintage. The monks had a great
advantage over the modern gardener in so far as
they could almost always site their herb garden
within a sunny walled courtyard. This not only
provided a warm, sheltered environment con-
ducive to happy, healthy growth, but also enhanced the warmth and fragrance of the air.
Unfortunately we can rarely offer plants those
conditions today, but we can help recreate them as
far as possible by establishing our traditional herb
garden in as sheltered a position as possible. Even
the presence of a south- or west-facing wall can
have a profound influence.

The situation is important in the successful
raising of herbs as well as providing the right
atmosphere. This is also provided by the layout of
the garden and the materials used to contain the
individual groups of plants. The original herb
gardens were constructed with clean walkways
isolating small beds containing each herb. These
paths were made of brick or unglazed tile, often in
intricate and symbolic patterns.

TRADITIONAL HERB GARDENS

To make an authentic herb garden of this period
you must refer back to history books and then
make patterned walkways similar to those described in the early literature. Providing the modern
material used is not too garish, a satisfactory result
can be obtained. Of course, for the real flavour of
the period it is necessary to be selective in the herbs
which you are going to grow. Those of North
American origin and many with homelands in Asia
would not have been seen in early monastery
gardens but it depends how authentic you wish to

An attractive group: mint and the
yellow flowers of tansy are backed
by the taller dill (left) and borage,
with, at the front, anise (left) and
parsley

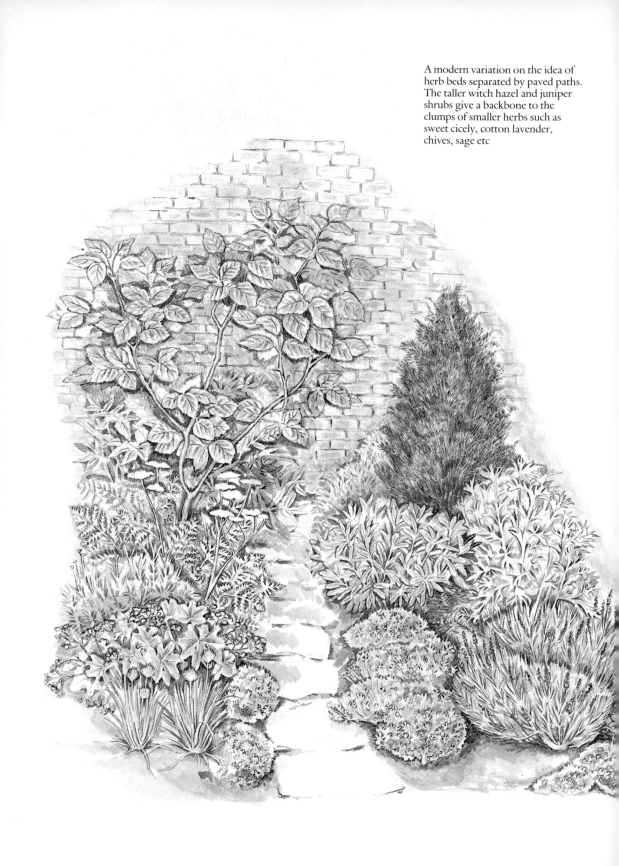

A modern variation on the idea of herb beds separated by paved paths. The taller witch hazel and juniper shrubs give a backbone to the clumps of smaller herbs such as sweet cicely, cotton lavender, chives, sage etc

be. I prefer a compromise, and while rejecting blatantly modern materials for the paths, I am quite happy with herbs from outside the period, providing that they are not too far removed by modern plant breeding from the typical herbs of that time.

The arrangement by which herbs were separated from one another was usually on a mathematical principle. Small beds would be created at regular intervals in a pattern of squares or circles, taller plants would be placed towards the centre and shorter ones to the outside. Where herbs were grown for medicinal purposes, certainly in the early apothecaries' gardens, cultivation seemed to be more earnest and the arrangement was very practical with the same strict regimenting, but less elaborate paving. In many cases these plants were grown in long beds about 1m (3ft) wide, each variety being separated by a paving stone or stones. The paths between the beds were also about a metre wide and constructed of paving stones. Visually uninteresting, this method of cultivation was clean and efficient and has much to commend it for a small courtyard garden where space is limited, or a long, narrow, difficult plot. The fact that it was primarily a means of cultivating medicinal plants is of little account. It is equally

successful for those for culinary use.

Many people feel that tradition should not be compromised, but in the case of the herb garden where the guide lines for tradition are already a little hazy, I think that it is permissible, especially when a much more appealing result will ensue. If you have a reasonable sized area that is sheltered, sunny, and approximately square in outline, then a cartwheel arrangement can be contrived. This design has a central focal point which forms the hub of the wheel and square or oblong divided beds providing the spokes. A rim is not practical, as one must be able to walk between the spokes and around the hub to enjoy or pick the plants. The

Grouping herbs in the border. The tall clumps of angelica and pink spikes of foxgloves provide height, and spill forward to prevent too much regularity. The smaller herbs include lavender (*centre right*), the yellow flowers of cotton lavender at each end, the grey foliage of wormwood, a mauve edging of thyme and the pink flowers of chives

hubs and spokes can be beds cut out of turf, but this requires a great deal of maintenance. It may look more appealing than paving or brick paths but these are hard wearing and easier to look after and the reflected heat from such materials benefits the plants and enhances their summer fragrance. When planting such a feature the herbs selected should be of fairly uniform height and not too tall. Each increasingly larger circle created by the spokes should be planted with the same herb to give a truly uniform effect. Choose plants like cotton lavender, hyssop and thyme for the best effect. They should be regularly trimmed so that strict formality is observed.

Imaginative designs using paving and brick paths. These are
hard wearing and easier to look after than turf

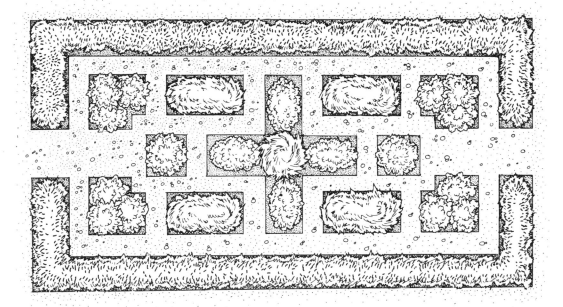

Traditional mathematical designs. Use herbs as the bold divisions with gravel between,
or use all herbs of varying stature. Bold lines are best created with lavender,
cotton lavender and hyssop; thyme, chervil and parsley are useful for filling in

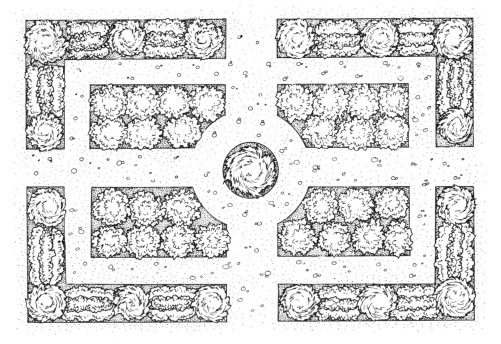

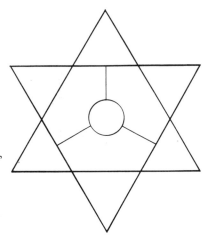

In the early days of herb gardening, signs of pagan or religious symbolism were often used. The traditional star design is outstanding when surrounded by well-raked gravel. Here, variegated sage in the centre is surrounded by three different thymes

The herbal ladder is an adaptation from the traditional arrangement for growing medicinal herbs. For the best effect, the rungs of the ladder should be narrow strips of turf, but gravel requires much less maintenance

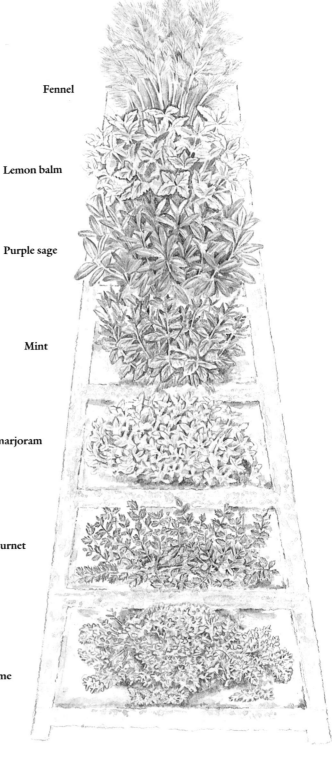

Fennel

Lemon balm

Purple sage

Mint

Golden marjoram

Burnet

Golden lemon thyme

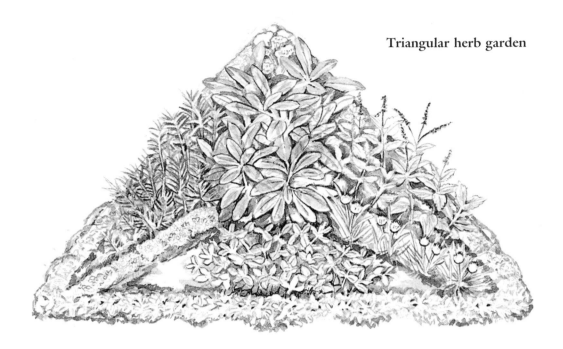

Triangular herb garden

Triquetra design

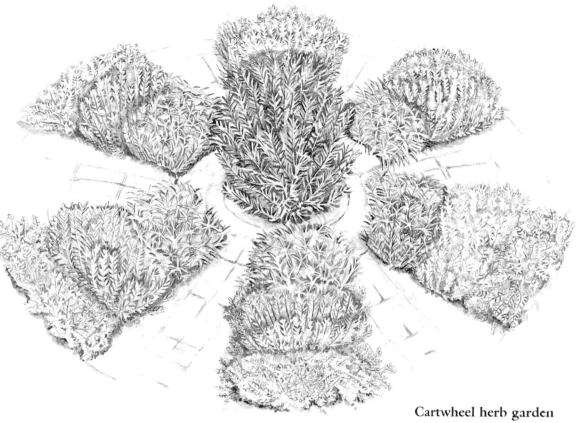

Cartwheel herb garden

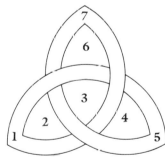

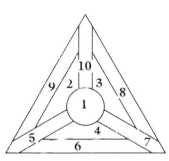

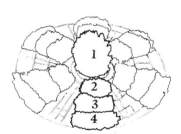

Triangular herb garden

A triangular herb garden provides an ideal focal point where paths converge, or on a difficult corner site

1 Sage
2 Tarragon
3 Mint.
4 Marjoram
5 Thyme
6 Basil
7 Chives
8 Thyme
9 Winter savory
10 Parsley

Triquetra design

The triquetra is an eyecatching traditional design which can be both beautiful and functional when filled with culinary herbs. For the best effect, surround with gravel or lawn

1 Chives
2 Mint
3 Sage
4 Rosemary
5 Thyme
6 Marjoram
7 Parsley

Cartwheel herb garden

This circular herb garden is arranged like a cartwheel, with the planting becoming progressively smaller towards the edge. This kind of feature is particularly attractive when there is room for a central ornament or sundial

1 Rosemary
2 Cotton lavender
3 Hyssop
4 Golden lemon thyme

FORMAL HERB GARDENS

In looking at the traditional style of herb garden, we have already covered several possibilities for a formal arrangement. The innovative gardener can do much more, however, for many herbs lend themselves to manicuring and can become mathematically precise parts of an intricately patterned design. Cotton lavender and hyssop clip well into small, low formal hedges and can be utilised to great effect. Similarly the smaller lavenders and rosemary can also be trimmed and bay grown into a shaped specimen of topiary. With such plants available and a wealth of ground-hugging subjects such as the prostrate thymes and pennyroyal to hand, quite elaborate and colourful designs can be executed.

Knot gardens, after the fashion of those created during Elizabethan times, can be made with herbs. Cotton lavender or hyssop can be used to provide low scrolled hedges, filled in between with coloured gravels, or low-growing herbs. Providing that maintenance is of a high standard, this type of herb garden design can be a constant source of pleasure. Indeed, it is a theme that can be adapted to the old Victorian carpet-bedding scheme. This involves the planting of herbs with contrasting flower and foliage colours in pre-determined patterns, often in such a way that a picture is created. Not whole-heartedly to be recommended for herb gardening, it is possible to extract parts of this technique and adapt it for herb growing. Illustrations can only rarely be successfully made using herb plants, but attractive patterns and pleasing colour combinations can be arranged without too much trouble.

Ensure that the plot is of sufficient size to take the bold blocks of colour necessary to make this form of garden a success. Anything much less than 10m (11yd) square is going to be unsuitable unless you intend to use a very limited selection of herbs. In selecting plants it is essential that they are

Herbal knot gardens have been part of gardening tradition for centuries. Not all of the spaces between the low hedges need to be filled with plants – they are equally attractive when left as gravel. Low hedges can be made with lavender, hyssop or cotton lavender

Tudor herb garden, with low
hedges similar to the knot garden.
The areas between the hedges are
best filled with ground hugging
subjects like shepherd's thyme or
pennyroyal

The traditional herbal maze of the
seventeenth century used rosemary,
lavender or rue for the hedges, but
rosemary and rue would not be
reliable at Harlow Car through the
winter. Hyssop and cotton lavender
can be used instead

suitable for trimming regularly to maintain a tight
pattern, they must be perennial, preferably
shrubby, and if possible evergreen or semi-
evergreen, for example the coloured leafed sages,
lavender and various species of santolina as well as
hyssop. The two most vital ingredients for success,
however, are first-class soil preparation and sufficient plants of good quality to provide the required
planting density from the outset. If a carpet-
bedding effect is required the herbs must be
planted at half their regular planting distances and
the plants cannot be picked for culinary purposes.
Such designs are purely visual fragrant delights.

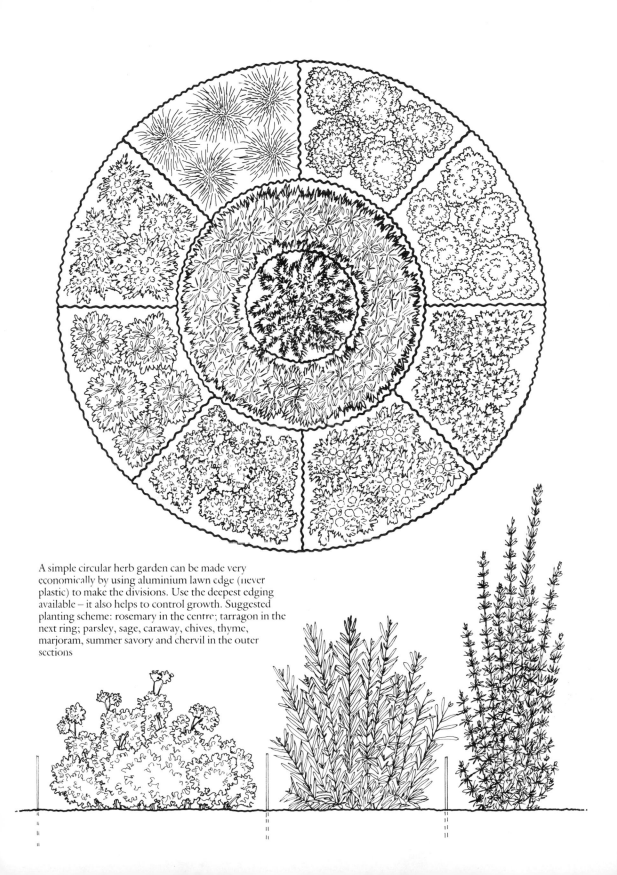

A simple circular herb garden can be made very economically by using aluminium lawn edge (never plastic) to make the divisions. Use the deepest edging available – it also helps to control growth. Suggested planting scheme: rosemary in the centre; tarragon in the next ring; parsley, sage, caraway, chives, thyme, marjoram, summer savory and chervil in the outer sections

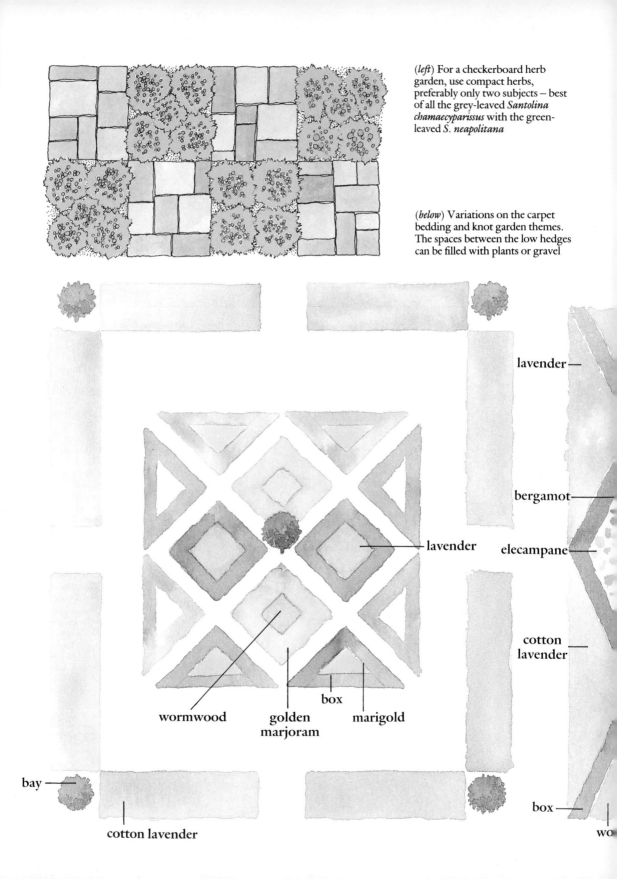

(*left*) For a checkerboard herb garden, use compact herbs, preferably only two subjects – best of all the grey-leaved *Santolina chamaecyparissus* with the green-leaved *S. neapolitana*

(*below*) Variations on the carpet bedding and knot garden themes. The spaces between the low hedges can be filled with plants or gravel

lavender —

bergamot—

elecampane —

lavender

cotton lavender

wormwood

golden marjoram

box

marigold

bay —

cotton lavender

box —

wo

Apart from traditional formal arrangements, another design that can be both attractively formal and useful in terms of a small leafy harvest, is the military arrangement. This, like the carpet-bedding type, depends upon shapes, essentially mathematical ones, with bold sweeps of a single herb surrounded by a continuous low hedge. Cotton lavender can be used throughout to designate the areas and bold plants of the upright form of rosemary can punctuate the edge or mark the four corners. Lavenders and sages can provide other

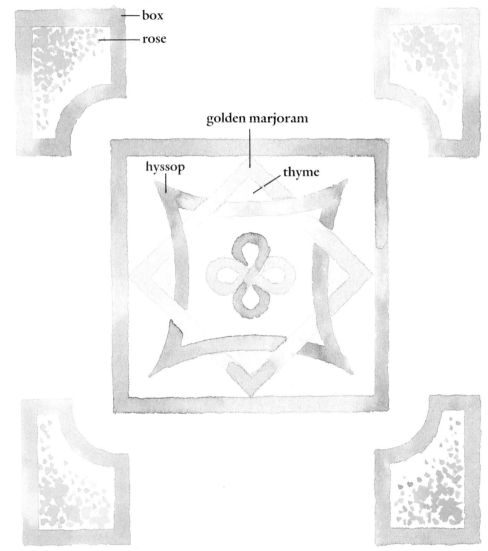

box

rose

golden marjoram

hyssop

thyme

components, remaining largely unclipped, but having their blossoms removed. The military-style herb garden, with its columnar 'soldiers', can be as large or as small as you care to make it, the number and frequency of rosemary 'sentries' being in accordance with the expanse of garden to be 'guarded'. This form of garden should be surrounded by a gravel path rather than grass, and is one which responds to the tasteful use of statuary in its centre.

INFORMAL HERB GARDENS

Many gardeners have only vague notions when it comes to the informal garden design. Tangled informality does not just happen, it has to be contrived. Almost as much effort has to be put into assembling an informal design, as in creating one of a formal nature. Not only have the cultural and visual aspects to be compatible, but unlike the formal herb garden, the diversity of plant material available for use in an informal setting is much greater. A wider knowledge of the growth and habit of herbs is absolutely essential. Rather than being the easy option the uninitiated might believe, the informal herb garden is more difficult to achieve than the regimented plantings of a formal arrangement.

The most successful informal arrangement for herbs follows the same lines as advocated for herbaceous perennial plants. Within a border the plants are either arranged against the background of a wall, fence or hedge, in which case the taller growing subjects are planted at the rear, or alternatively the border is viewed from either side with the bigger plants in the centre. The island bed is intended to be viewed from all around and therefore taller herbs must be placed in the centre with shorter plants radiating out to the edge. While most people's idea of an island bed is circular, there is no reason why it should not be oval or kidney-shaped. Nor need it be placed in a lawn. Herbs when grown on the island system look quite stunning when surrounded by paving or a broad sweep of fine gravel.

Groups of five to seven plants of a kind are necessary to give the bold effect that is desired. Informality tempts the plant collector, so if you have to collect a wide variety, do so in quantity. The only situation that I know of where you can get away with spotty planting is if you have limited space for a few herbs near the back door, or you wish to create a corner for the bees. The wildlife

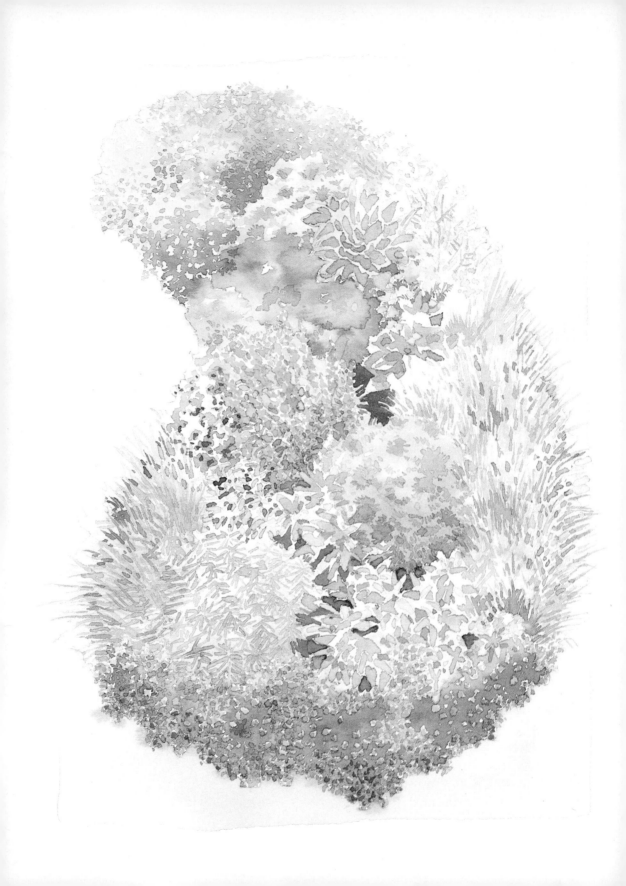

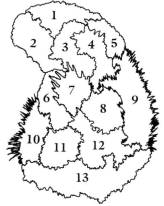

(*left*) Herbs and fragrant garden flowers create an attractive island bed

1 Thyme	8 Southernwood
2 Lemon thyme	9 Lavender
3 Wormwood	10 Pinks
4 Comfrey	11 Tarragon
5 Curry plant	12 Bergamot
6 White violets	13 Wall
7 Foxgloves	germander

(*below*) A happy arrangement of annual and perennial garden flowers and herbs. The subtle green of the herbs highlights the pink lilies and yellow marigolds. The mauve borage (*left and top*) and purple sage (*centre*) add to the richness and depth of colour

garden is extremely popular just now and demands wide diversity if you are to keep bees coming all summer.

Choose a sunny corner and plant the herbs as tastefully as possible. If the area is very small it will have to be individual plants, but if there is enough room, plant in groups of three. An arrangement that is intended to attract insect life will essentially be grown for its flowers – catmint, marjoram, borage, and thyme for example, so informality is very much the keynote. Flowers need not be excluded from other kinds of informal herb garden, but when good quality foliage is desired the flowers have to be sacrificed. If you find that this is likely to be the case and the visual effect is suffering, then introduce a generous number of good flowering herbs that were once used for perfumery or medicinal purposes. Try monkshood, clove carnation or hemp agrimony, and do not neglect the show that can be provided by pot marigolds and nasturtiums.

Unfortunately not all of us are able to devote

sufficient space to a herb garden. We might be able to utilise containers and window boxes, but their use is restricted to certain varieties that will respond to that kind of cultivation. Fortunately most of the important culinary kinds do, but it leaves a vast array that the enthusiastic herb grower cannot successfully accommodate. That is, unless he integrates them with his other plantings. There is no reason at all why herbs should not be mixed with other garden plants, especially in the mixed border where shrubs, herbaceous plants and bulbs mingle together. Some gardeners even claim that the association of certain plants together is beneficial to one or both. This is called companion planting. It is possible that by putting certain plants together, pests that formerly attacked the popular garden subject will be kept away by the presence of certain herbs. For example, planting chives amongst roses to ward off attacks of greenfly is now common practice, and the use of both garlic and pot marigold in the vegetable garden for similar pest controls is gaining a footing.

HERB GARDENING IN CONTAINERS

If you are unable to grow herbs in the open ground for lack of space, or even if you prefer them close at hand by the kitchen door, then container cultivation is for you. There are many containers that can be used, some specifically intended for plants, others not, yet sufficiently versatile to be used successfully. However good containers are they do suffer limitations even when you have prepared a suitable compost. Compost and drainage are half the problem with growing herbs. The main constraint, however, is the limitation upon what can be grown. It is no use trying to accommodate lovage and angelica in modern garden containers or window boxes, they just will not flourish. Apart from looking ungainly, they will not produce good, crisp, healthy foliage when their roots are restricted and they are short of moisture. Irrespective of how diligent you are about watering it is difficult to give such large plants sufficient when grown in a modern planter.

Which Container?

Before choosing the herbs we must look at the containers which can be used. Window boxes are all very similar, but do select the deepest one that you can afford or accommodate. Not only has the box to tie in physically and visually with the building to which it is to be attached, but its weight when laden with plants and damp compost must be considered. Of course, light-weight peat- and sand-based soil-less compost can be used to reduce weight, but these are not as suitable as the soil-based John Innes potting composts for longer term perennial herbs like thyme, mint and chives. If there are no constraints upon the kind of window box which you can choose, then the ideal would be at least 30cm (1ft) wide and 25cm (10in) deep. This would allow most of the popular culinary herbs to be grown without too regular disturbance. Not only must the volume of compost which the box will hold be substantial, but the facility for drainage must be good. Drainage holes are essential, even though window boxes are given to drying out quickly. If you have a window box with no facility for drainage, you will have to create it yourself. This means scattering a generous layer of gravel or broken pots several centimetres deep all along the base of the box to provide temporary alleviation from waterlogging. Not only is this much less effective than drainage holes, but valuable compost space is occupied by the drainage medium.

The same applies to troughs and patio planters. Good drainage is essential. Much of what applies to window boxes will also hold true for these. Containers of any kind must be able to hold sufficient volume of compost to accommodate plant growth successfully. Within the scope of what is visually appealing, it can safely be said that the larger the container the better. Large volumes of compost dry out more slowly and heat up at a slower rate on hot summer days. They do have disadvantages however. When used for growing plants of doubtful hardiness – like bay trees – they are more difficult to move to the safety of a porch or unheated greenhouse at the approach of winter and the tendency is to leave them where they are to take a chance. By being in a container the plant has its roots exposed to frosting and is much more vulnerable to winter damage than if planted in the open ground.

There is a popular misconception that if plants are growing in a large container the soil is not so rapidly depleted of nutrients, nor its structure so quickly destroyed. This has a tiny element of truth in it, but by and large it is a myth. The compost in a large container should receive attention as promptly as that in a small container for there are, proportionately, more plants in the large vessel.

Apart from conventional garden containers there are others that can be successfully used. The

A traditional strawberry pot planted with culinary herbs; chives, thyme and parsley planted in an attractive spiral arrangement

Herbs in the mixed border, providing a varied and fragrant leafy foil for colourful border plants

1 Foxgloves
2 Southernwood or wormwood
3 Purple loosestrife
4 Thyme
5 Woad
6 Sage
7 Pinks
8 Cotton lavender
9 Chives

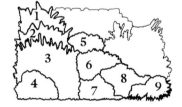

strawberry pot, in a slightly altered form, is now sold as a herb pot too. These may be up to 1m (3ft) tall, the most attractive ones being made of clay, but quite serviceable pieces are now produced in plastic. They look rather like tall, elegant, curved chimney pots with a large hole at the top and a series of smaller ones down the sides. Rather than being mere holes, these are made as pockets, each one capable of accommodating a plant. The idea is that most of the pot is hidden by the foliage burgeoning from the pockets and the summit. The roots all penetrate the central mass of compost. This works for a number of small herbs if planted when quite young. Transplanted seedlings or well rooted cuttings are the best material to start with. Plant them systematically from the lower pockets upwards, filling the pot with compost as you go. If you attempt to fill the pot first and then put the plants in, you will be in difficulty. For firm planting it is essential to have one hand inside the pot to control the operation. Strawberry or herb pots are perfect for what I call herbal kitchen pots. Crown the pot with sage and fill the pockets equally with parsley, thyme and chives in a spiralled arrangement. Not only does the pot look very appealing, but it is productive too.

Half barrels are also good for miniature herb gardens and give the whole feature a rustic look. Try planting sage boldly in the centre and parsley, chives and thyme around the edge in an informal arrangement. If using recently discarded vinegar or whisky casks, then it is a wise precaution to scrub them thoroughly inside before use. There is rarely any contamination of the compost, but when there is, the whole barrel has to be turned out and a fresh start made.

There is no such risk when using an old sink. Although not too attractive visually, old glazed sinks do make excellent containers for growing herbs. If you really object to the glaze, then it is perfectly possible to give it a more natural look by

MAKING HYPERTUFA

Hypertufa is a material which can be made by the gardener to simulate the properties of natural tufa (a porous stone material). In its wet mixed state it can be moulded to disguise unsightly containers, such as old sinks, and looks quite natural. Soft, yet resilient, it can be sculpted when necessary and provides a pleasing background for the plants.

There are different views as to how much of each ingredient should be used in the mixture. I favour the traditional mixture of three parts by volume of river sand, two parts by volume sedge peat and one part cement. This is mixed with water until the agglomeration is sufficiently stiff that when a shovel is pushed repeatedly into it, the ridges that are produced remain. If they collapse, the mixture is too wet, if they do not form properly and crumble it is too dry. When suitably mixed, it can be trowelled on to a sink or other containers and an appropriate finish can be created. If the sink or container is glazed, then it is wise to coat it with a household adhesive prior to dressing with hypertufa.

While the ingredients in the mixture are all essential, variation in quantities will yield a mix with different properties and shades of colour. If the mixture does not appear to be bonding satisfactorily, add a little more cement, but not too much, for an excess of cement will lead to the cracking and crazing of the surface when the hypertufa has dried out.

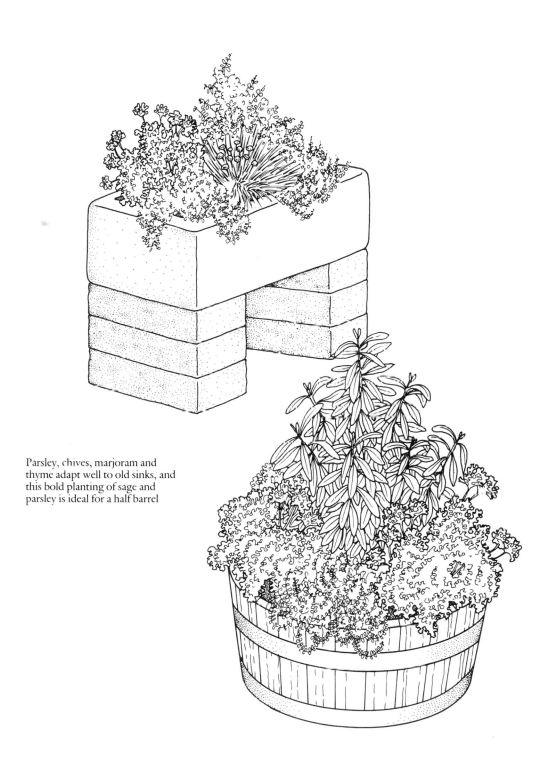

Parsley, chives, marjoram and
thyme adapt well to old sinks, and
this bold planting of sage and
parsley is ideal for a half barrel

applying a peat, sand and cement mixture called hypertufa. Its mixture and application is described in most alpine gardening books. Marjoram, thyme, parsley and chives all adapt well to such conditions. Drainage is good if the plug is removed and the hole covered with metal gauze. If raised off the ground on brick or stone piers, water can drain away freely and the sink is at a more convenient level. At about 60cm (2ft) off the ground it does not lose its visual appeal and both weeding and garnering the harvest are easier tasks.

Small herb gardens can be made in many odd containers. Old car tyres stacked upon one another, painted white and filled with compost create an unusual and not unpleasant spectacle. I have seen herb gardens in large hollowed-out logs, old wheel-barrows. toilet pans and old baths. However, most gardeners who are going to grow herbs in containers purchase those used to accommodate summer bedding plants or spring flowering bulbs. These are perfectly adequate, but remember that even the larger containers hold only a relatively small body of compost and plants that are going to overwinter need some protection if they are to survive. Either the container needs removing to a light and more or less frost-free place, or else it must be well protected with sacks or straw. If your containers are made of any kind of pottery material, they and their contents must be given frost-free winter conditions or else they are likely to fracture.

Which Herbs?

There are no hard and fast rules about what you can or cannot plant in a container, other than the constraints of size. It is good fun to experiment and see what you can get away with. Annual plants are especially amenable and if you make a mistake it can quickly be rectified. With perennial herbs you should be a little more cautious, especially if the container is to be a feature on the patio or by the

Nothing is more delightful than relaxing on the patio surrounded by pots of herbal fragrance. Many popular and colourful kinds respond to pot culture if their watering needs are carefully attended to. Seen here are (*from top, clockwise*) purple sage, yarrow, chives with thyme, giant chives, and sage

back door. Initially choose reliable kinds like lavender, rosemary, thyme, parsley, mint and marjoram. One of my favourite combinations is of lavender or rosemary as a centrepiece with various thymes lending support. This is a reliable and more or less evergreen arrangement which I think of as a scented or fragrant pot. Culinary containers can bristle with chives, parsley and thyme, or flowering herb containers with marjoram, thyme and soapwort. The themes that one can adopt are nearly as diverse as the plant combinations. However, bear in mind that while planters are merely a substitute for the open garden for many herbs, they are the only reliable way of cultivating a number of other very desirable types outside in Britain. These include the various basils and anise as well as the shrubby common myrtle. If you have to garden with containers, then take advantage of all its benefits.

This applies to the window box too. Although giving the gardener more constraints than the container or planter by virtue of its long narrow profile, it does have the benefit of not only being an excellent place in which to grow smaller herbs, especially annuals and biennials, but also a first-class nursery. Even if you have room for herbs in the open garden, do consider the possibilities of the window box as a small propagation unit.

Most window boxes, however, have to serve more than a nursery role. For flats and many town houses they are the only herb garden and it is more satisfactory to purchase ready grown seedlings or rooted cuttings rather than attempt to raise the plants yourself. If you do wish to raise your own herbs from seed it is better to do so on the kitchen window sill and then transfer the plants to the window box. Trying to use a window box for all the stages of growth is futile and wastes both time and productive space. The plant combinations which can be used in window boxes are almost as diverse as for containers. For the most part small plants should be used because their foliage must not be permitted to grow up and exclude light from the window, while at the same time the small amount of compost available means that only shorter growing subjects are likely to prosper. I like to arrange a window box with taller herbs like fennel at each end, while filling the middle of the box with smaller kinds like thyme, parsley and marjoram, the whole soil area being covered with a creeping thyme which can be allowed to trail over the edges of the box. All except the fennel can be allowed to flower. Fennel would get too tall and the foliage would fade. Such a box is a colourful, fragrant and useful addition to the garden.

HERB GARDENING INDOORS
Everyone can enjoy this kind of herb gardening irrespective of gardening expertise. All that you need is a light, airy window sill and a little enthusiasm. Nowadays a whole range of specially prepared packs including seeds, containers and compost are offered. While not decrying their usefulness, particularly in attracting the attention of non-gardeners to the possibilities offered by herb growing, it is cheaper and better to shop around individually for the materials and seeds which you need. But before doing this you need to know what can be successfully cultivated indoors. Most herbs can be grown to a limited extent, only being restricted by the size of the pot. However, it is better to select varieties that will grow well from the outset – the group loosely referred to as pot herbs. This includes pot marjoram, basil, thyme, parsley and most of the smaller kitchen herbs which the cook needs to pluck all of the time.

Herbs that are unsuited to indoor cultivation are the taller vigorous kinds and most of those with hairy or downy leaves. These particularly object to the conditions that prevail in most kitchens, such as a hot steamy atmosphere where moisture will settle on their foliage and cause various fungal leaf spots

69

HERBS FOR THE KITCHEN WINDOW SILL

These are the herbs loosely referred to as pot herbs and which are tolerant of a warm steamy atmosphere.

Anise

Basil
(Sweet and Bush)

Chervil

Chives

Marjoram
(Sweet and Pot)

Mint
(Spearmint and Peppermint)

Parsley

Summer Savory

Tarragon

Thyme

to develop. If left untreated, brown, fading foliage will lead to the dying-back of young shoots. If you must grow herbs with downy foliage indoors, then ensure that they are provided with as dry and hot a position as possible. This even applies to common sage, although with care it is possible to grow it reasonably well in the kitchen where it is most needed. For the finest foliage though, it must be grown elsewhere.

Indoor cultivation of herbs does not necessarily mean that the plants must be restricted to pots, although this is the simplest method. There are a number of very good indoor troughs and planters available nowadays. While many merely act as containers for serried ranks of pots it is possible, with some, to plant them up like a window box. This works well where plants that have similar compost requirements can be accommodated and where one species is not going to take over the entire planter. But this is not the best way for the novice to start. Get to know your plants first and then graduate to this kind of indoor herb gardening. When skilfully executed it is a delight, but I have seen more horrors than delights!

Pot culture is really the best method for productive herb gardening, but that does not mean that you have to be unimaginitive in displaying your plants. Providing that they are going to receive adequate light, they can be displayed in much the same manner as indoor plants. I enjoy growing them in pots inserted through rings distributed evenly up a free-standing stem. Modern plastic hanging planters can also be used and often incorporate a self-watering device. You can have a row of herbs along the kitchen window sill and another suspended along the top of the window. As long as they receive sufficient light they will be happy. Indoor gardening may not offer the same opportunities for raising a wide range of herbs as gardening in the open, but there are still sufficient challenges to satisfy the most ardent gardener.

A window box full of culinary herbs is a delight – the most popular kitchen herbs respond well to this kind of cultivation. This box has fennel at each end, with smaller culinary herbs in the centre and creeping thyme spilling over the edge. NB Normally, fennel should not be allowed to flower as it would become too tall for the window box

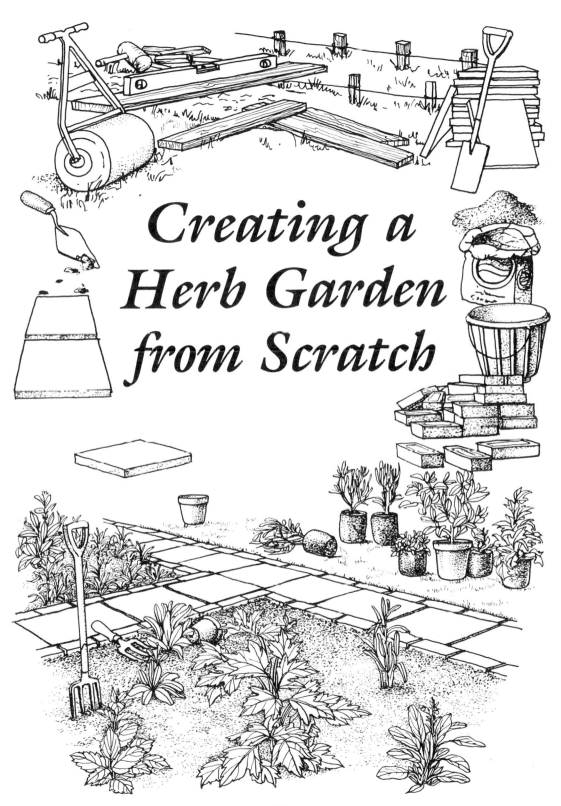

Creating a
Herb Garden
from Scratch

*I*RRESPECTIVE of the size or shape that your herb garden is going to be, soil preparation and path construction are going to follow along broadly similar lines. Resist the temptation of trying to create an instant herb garden – there is no such thing. Ideally you should be planning ahead during the summer of one year for planting in the spring of the next. It will be two summers ahead before your vision will be anywhere near fulfilment.

LEVELLING THE SITE

If a formal herb feature is to be of any size, then proper levelling of the site is vital. A mathematical arrangement which looks perfect from above becomes a nonsense on uneven ground. Measure out the allocated area using an existing feature as your fixed point from which all measurements are taken. Use pegs and string to mark the outline of the plot and if square corners are necessary make a simple wooden construction to ensure that you get them at right angles. Strong pieces of planed timber can be used to make a simple square based upon the Pythagoras theory (sides in the ratio of 3:4 and the cross piece 5). A square corner can be adjusted using string, but a wooden square makes life so much easier. Having established the area on the ground with stakes and string, put in several stout permanent marker stakes at prominent places.

Unless you are very lucky the ground will be full of bumps and hollows. It may look more or less flat, but once level pegs are put in, they will more likely reveal wide discrepancies. It is better that this is discovered at an early stage so that something can be done about it. Select the highest point, take a strong peg and knock it to within 1cm of ground level. You will need a good straight plank which can be rested lying on its edge on top of that stake, so that the level can be transferred to other pegs at strategic points over the plot. A spirit level used on the top edge of the board will ensure reasonable accuracy with the levels. When moving across a plot with stakes and board, slight discrepancies will creep in, but these can be ignored unless you are gardening on a very large scale where they will make a discernible difference. In the average garden, the simple method described is perfectly adequate. By attaching a tight string around the top of each peg and linking one with another, a reasonable idea of levels can be attained.

Having found out what your levels are is one thing, but it is quite another deciding how to cope with discrepancies. For the most part a compromise between the lower level and the higher one is the easiest to achieve without disrupting the adjacent garden too much. Select a peg that is midway between the higher and lower levels. Cut a short strong stick that is the exact length of the exposed portion of the peg that is to act as the mean level. Then start to redistribute the soil, holding this short measuring stick against each peg

Levelling: **a & b** Use pegs and string to mark the plot, making sure the corners are square; **c** put in strong pegs at the same level, using a plank and spirit level; **d** cut a short measuring stick to use as a guide when redistributing soil

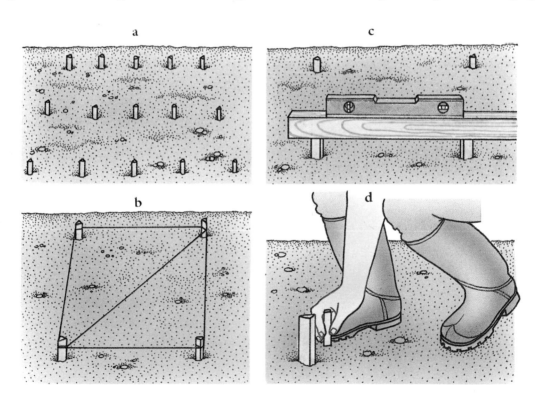

75

to indicate when either sufficient soil has been added or removed. This is only a rough and ready means of attaining a level site, for the ground is likely to be tight and compacted in the areas where soil has been removed and therefore stable, whereas in built-up parts it will be loose and puffy and likely to settle later. However, it does bring some order to the site and even if it proves to be impractical to level evenly, it is possible, using similar methods, to create a gentle slope which makes life much easier for the succeeding stages of development.

PREPARING THE SOIL

It depends very much upon site conditions as to what you do now. If the soil is raw and relatively weed-free then go ahead and lay paths. Otherwise you must dig the entire area thoroughly. It may be tempting to lay a brick or paved path upon firm bare earth, but if there is couch grass or bindweed lurking in the soil it will merely be paved over and will then creep sideways amongst the herbs so that no matter how diligently you weed it will return. The paths will act as protection for a permanent reservoir of pernicious creeping rootstocks that will be all but impossible to eliminate. Although it might be satisfying to get on with the job and get the paving laid, in the longer term careful and thorough soil preparation will bring its rewards.

It is best to dig the soil thoroughly during the late summer or early autumn, for then it will have an opportunity to be weathered during the winter months. Before turning the first spadeful, check that the site is not likely to become waterlogged. If in any doubt provide a drain of some kind before digging begins. As most herb gardens are not too large an elaborate drainage system is unlikely to be required. It is ideal if a drain can be laid though the area and attached to an existing land drain, but perfectly adequate if excess water can be taken to a soakaway. This need merely be a pit filled with hardcore into which two or three drains from different areas of the plot empty. The drains need not even be piped, although it would be better if they were. A trench about 25cm (10in) wide and 30cm (1ft) deep below the first full spit of soil, filled with coarse gravel or clinker, will usually do the job.

Digging can now commence. Do not be tempted to knock down the soil and make it crumbly, but leave it in big clods so that the weather can get at it. All weed cover should be buried. If you leave any vestige of green poking out, the plant will start growing again. Troublesome perennial weeds like dandelion, couchgrass and bindweed must be removed by hand during the digging process. This will inevitably mean that some of the larger lumps have to be knocked down to extract the roots. Where the task seems impossible because of the sheer quantity of perennial weeds, turn the soil over and allow the weed to sprout. When it is shooting lustily, spray the foliage with a systemic herbicide based upon glyphosate. This does not contaminate the soil, but is absorbed by the foliage and translocated around the sap stream of the plant. It takes two or three weeks before it appears to be working and you see the whole plant dying even though the weedkiller only touched the foliage. Where weeds have a strong hold and an extensive rootstock it is the easiest way of eliminating them. However, it must be applied during the growing period to be fully effective.

Herbs prefer a lean hungry soil rather than one which is rich in organic matter and during their growth period it is better to give them an occasional liquid feed rather than have them growing in a rich organic medium. Except on the most impoverished of soils it is unnecessary to incorporate well rotted garden compost or animal manure during the digging operation. The only time that I would consider it desirable would be on a very dry sandy soil when the addition of a little organic matter would help retain moisture. This can also be done in other ways using various inorganic soil additives.

I have used two materials with success, both more or less permanent in their action, but rather expensive. However, considering their permanency the investment is very worthwhile. Perlite is a white granular substance mined in the Greek Islands which, when heated, looks rather like granular polystyrene. This is used extensively for propagation work, either alone or mixed with peat as a rooting medium. Most gardeners are familiar with the finer grades of this material, but there is a coarser sort that is used for soil conditioning. The other material has similar properties and is used in just the same way. Introduced as arcillite a few years ago, this is a montmorillinite clay mined in the United States and prepared in such a way that it looks like crushed up plant pot. Both materials have a high water absorption capacity. On light soils this is beneficial as rain passes through these quickly. The soil additive absorbs much of what falls and retains it until the surrounding sand particles begin to dry up. A similar phenomenon happens with clay soils which become easier to work even after heavy rain by virtue of the fact that the soil additive is retaining much of the excess water. As the soil dries out moisture is released, thereby extending the period before the surface begins to crack. Either material can be introduced while digging, the best results being obtained by adding 25 per cent by volume to the area being dug. This may seem rather a lot, but once fully integrated into the soil it will make it as near perfect as possible for most of the herbs which we will consider. Once you have conditioned the soil in this way it is permanent. Some of the additive will obviously be washed into the lower reaches of the soil, but an occasional handful of fresh material sprinkled over the surface will keep it topped up.

LAYING OUT THE HERB GARDEN

The plan is drawn up, the site level and thoroughly dug, so now the excitement can begin. The first features can be laid out on the bare soil. If we take the simplest informal designs, then little needs to be done except to mark out the areas designated as beds. You will obviously have an idea of the shapes that you want and these can be measured out using stakes to mark the closest and most distant points. A rope laid on the ground can be used to join the markers together, adjustments being made until the correct shape is achieved. Where a bed is being taken out of existing lawn this is the best way to determine the shape. All you need do then is to cut around the edge of the rope with an edging iron or spade and you will have your outline. It is very pleasant to have freedom of design but use it sensibly and give your herb bed sweeping arcs and circles rather than fussy niches and contortions. The latter make work and are difficult to maintain.

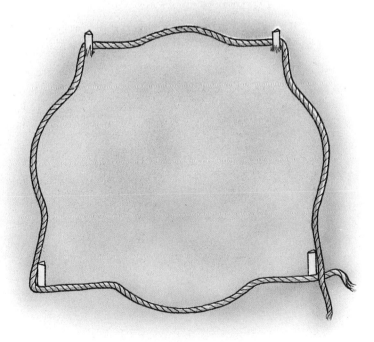

Formal herb gardens demand a little more patience and accuracy. Like the informal kind they should be marked out on the ground using stakes and strings initially, but replacing the strings on the main features with a line of sprinkled sand. Most formal herb gardens have hard paths and paved areas and these must be prepared for. The gardener rarely has an opportunity to lay his paths on solid ground. The area has usually been thoroughly cultivated and is very spongy. This means that laying paving or bricks directly on to the soil is impossible as they will twist and contort as soon as walked upon. A good foundation is required consisting of up to 20cm (8in) depth of brick or concrete rubble firmly rolled or tamped into the soil. A small vibrating roller will compact the base admirably and the minimal rental cost of this will be well repaid. There is nothing worse than laying an intricately patterned path on a base that sinks unevenly within a few weeks.

Mark out a formal herb garden with stakes and string, then use sand to mark out the main features

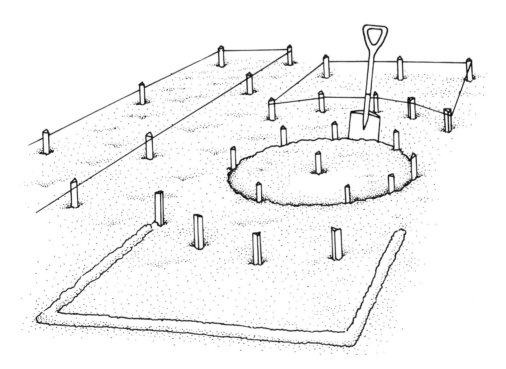

Once the hardcore base has been laid, a generous layer of sand should be spread over the top to even it up. If slabs are to be used, indicate the edges of the path using strings attached to stout pegs. The width of the path should be compatible with the size of paving slabs being used. There is no sense in making a path in which slabs have to be regularly cut in order to fit the layout. Some gardeners are confident enough to lay the slabs directly onto a bed of sand. This works if they are really large and heavy, but in the herb garden they are more likely to be of modest proportions and easy to dislodge if not firmly bedded on mortar. Use a mix of four parts by volume of river sand and one of cement and make little patches, one at each corner and one in the centre for the slabs to sit on. These will secure the paving sufficiently. When putting slabs down they must not only be laid square, but level as well. A board and spirit level are again vital to get the paving even and level in each direction.

Making a paved path. Make the base of firmed rubble, then add a generous layer of sand before bedding the slabs firmly on mortar

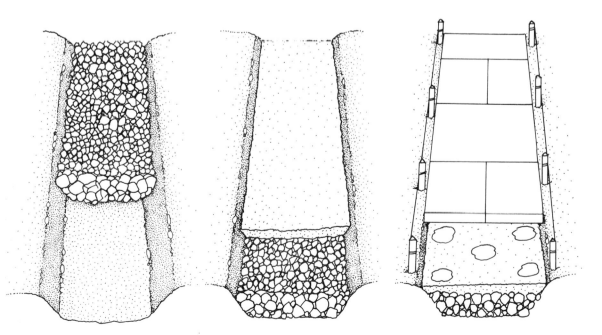

81

Less formal arrangements often use crazy paving with the idea that creeping scented plants like shepherd's thyme and pennyroyal can be grown in the cracks, scenting the air whenever trodden on. This is very nice in theory, but maintenance is high. It is much better to cement down the individual pieces of paving, filling the cracks between with a mortar mix, but leaving deliberate pockets at irregular intervals to accommodate sweet scented creeping plants. With bricks, cementing is vital if they are to become a solid even surface. Merely bedding on sand encourages unevenness.

PLANTING

For most herb gardens the paths provide the framework and it is into this that the picture is painted. However, the canvas will need a little touching up before the 'paint' is applied, because during path construction the beds will have been trampled. Fork these over lightly, removing any debris from the path-laying operations and then planting can start, beginning with the skeleton planting. This is peculiar to the formal layout where small hedges of herbs are planted to define areas. Apart from having sturdy plants of even growth, the essential for the production of a strong, even dwarf hedge is uniform soil. Pockets of variation in the soil will be reflected in the growth of the hedge.

Outlines having been prepared, the individual features are filled. Throughout the whole planting operation a series of plant spacing sticks should be employed, one for each kind of herb. Adhere rigidly to the distances intended. An uneven distribution of plants causes an uneven distribution of foliage which is difficult to disguise even when the plants are approaching maturity. If the shapes are complex and merely measuring out areas and marking them with sand is inadequate, then a wooden template can be employed. This is a shape which is placed on the ground and then filled with plants. On its removal the desired shape in plant material remains behind.

When doing the solid planting in a formal scheme, start from the centre and work outwards. This enables you to tidy up the soil around the plants that you have planted. The same applies with an informal layout. Such plantings should be marked out on the soil with lines of sand. Make them irregular, but sweeping and curving and allow some taller groups to impinge upon the area that might normally be occupied by shorter growing subjects. Although not as demanding as the mathematical precision of the formal herb garden, the presentation of the informal kind demands a greater artistic ability.

Most plants that are used in herb gardens spend their young lives growing in pots. Often their root systems will be congested and they will be pot bound, just waiting to get out into fresh soil. Where this is the case, do not merely knock the plant out of its pot and drop it in a hole in the soil, but help it to break out of its pot ball by splitting it open. Nothing too drastic, just run a sharp knife down the root ball in two or three places to allow the roots to escape into the fresh soil. This is absolutely vital with woody plants like rosemary and lavender. If not treated in this way, they will just sit in the soil and make little root. It may even be possible, after a year, to take hold of the plant and lift it out of the soil. A few root hairs may have created a little fuzz around the rootball, but the plant will have essentially been existing on its old rootball and the moisture that has percolated in from the surrounding soil.

Pot grown herbs that are in good order should be planted with as little root disturbance as possible. Even if the soil is damp in spring, it is vital that the plants are thoroughly watered before planting and watched until they are well established. In theory it is possible to establish a herb garden from pot grown plants at any time of the year, but spring is best. Soil conditions are moist, the plants are ready to burst into life and warmer weather is on the way. Planting during summer is fine, but you do create a watering problem. It takes a number of weeks in hot dry weather to get pot grown herbs established before artificial watering can be relaxed. If you plant during the autumn or winter the plants have little opportunity to establish themselves as the soil is so cold and uninviting. They may just as well be kept in their pots and protected from the winter climate. The only herbs that can be usefully planted during the winter – preferably with spring in sight – are the bare-rooted kinds. These include horseradish, salad burnet and comfrey, none of which respond very well to pot culture. When planting, trim off any excess or damaged roots and push the plants firmly into the soil. If frosts ensue, check periodically to see that the plants have not been lifted out of the soil and their roots exposed. If they have, wait for a break in the weather and firm them back in.

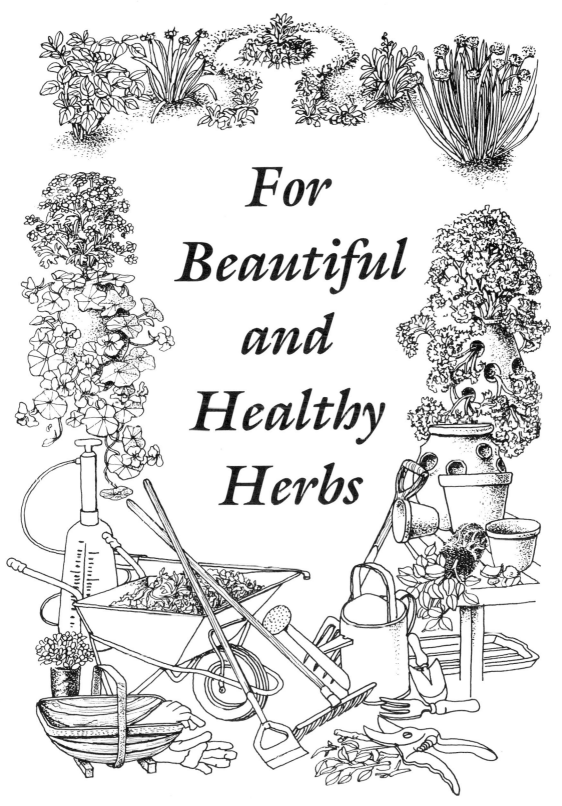

For
Beautiful
and
Healthy
Herbs

*H*ERB gardening is labour intensive. Annual weeds are a nuisance, but not impossible to control. It is the perennial kinds that are a nightmare, and while it is possible to selectively weedkill these when growing amongst established herb plants, the labour is disproportionate to the results achieved. So if you have inherited a weed-infested herb garden, propagate the best of your herbs and start again.

Weeding is the most constant task. As the plants are often used for cooking it is undesirable to use herbicides so weeding must be by hand. As the majority of the herbs commonly grown come from warm climates and demand well-drained soil conditions, mulching in the usual way with well-rotted garden compost or peat to suppress weeds is not practical. Fine grit or pea shingle can be used as a mulch and is quite effective. It helps to suppress weeds, looks in keeping with most herb plants and serves as a moisture conserving mulch, trapping moisture beneath and also providing its own as the cool stones attract condensation at night which then trickles between them.

Pruning is a necessity with all herb gardens, and spring pruning of all the shrubby herb plants is essential to maintain them in good order. It is much preferred to allowing the plant to develop and then cutting back into old wood. A framework of older wood is acceptable, but the young growths should spring from wood that is middle-aged rather than elderly. This can only be achieved with annual attention. While spring is the best time to prune in the informal herb garden, it is a continuous process in the formal garden, although in most cases it amounts to no more than regular clipping with shears. This can be done throughout the summer as needed, but do not clip after mid-August even if the plants get a little shaggy. A little superfluous growth provides protection for the plants during the winter.

Shrubby plants like sage should be trained from

an early date and be regularly pinched to encourage bushy growth. This will happen naturally when you harvest the fresh young foliage, but not at the outset. Young sage plants in particular have a tendency to produce a strong leading growth and will head on upwards if you do not remove this when about 10cm high. If you remove a large enough piece you can often root the shoot as a cutting. This applies also to other shrubby herbs like lavender and rosemary.

Apart from pruning, herbs require regular maintenance and grooming if they are to look smart and appealing. Regular weeding provides an opportunity for noticing and removing damaged and decaying stems or accumulations of old leaves. Unless the seeds are required for cooking, old flower heads should be removed as soon as they fade. As a general rule cut flower stems down to the base of the plant. With some varieties you will have to come to a decision as to whether you allow them to flower at all. Although very attractive, some plants, like sage, produce inferior foliage if allowed to flower, while for others, like chives, it seems to make little difference one way or the other.

IN AUTUMN AND WINTER

As autumn approaches the herb garden looks a sad and sorry place. Of all garden plants, herbs probably look the most forlorn after the first sharp frost, and this causes great concern to the new gardener in his first winter. Things are not as bad as they at first appear, for although all the annuals will have come to an end and the foliage of many perennial kinds has collapsed, if you scrape away a little soil at the base of permanent plants you will be able to see latent buds just waiting to outwit the winter and surge into growth once spring sunshine warms the soil again. These buds need protection, though not from the cold as they are perfectly hardy. Slugs and snails are a much greater menace and therefore no winter hiding places must be allowed to remain. Clear away all old plant debris which provides a winter haven for slugs and snails. As an added precaution put down a few slug pellets near vulnerable subjects like fennel. In the damp these pellets quickly spoil, so spread a few out at strategic intervals on a piece of slate or tile. Then cover with another piece, or a small upturned pot with a hole in the side, raising a small roof to allow protection from rain, but give access to the slugs. This is also a good way of preventing birds or pets from finding the pellets.

During winter the herb garden is at rest. The bare areas of soil left by departing annual herbs should be turned up to the elements, but apart from that all should be at peace.

SPRING IN THE HERB GARDEN
As spring arrives and the first green shoots appear, winter damage to the plants should be assessed and removed. Soil that has been compacted by heavy winter rain must be lightly pricked over with a garden fork. It is appropriate to feed the herb garden at this time, pricking the fertiliser in as you go. High nutrient fertilisers are not desirable, so for safety most gardeners opt for a medium grade of bonemeal. This has nutrients in the right balance to satisfy most herbs and being a slow-release fertiliser will be adequate for the entire growing season. As a dressing for most of the popular herbs, distribute about a teacupful to every square metre of soil, putting proportionally more of the fertiliser in the centre of clump forming plants like marjoram to prevent the middle of the plant from dying out.

MAINTAINING HERBS IN CONTAINERS
Obviously all that has gone before regarding planting, pruning, weeding and manicuring equally applies to herbs that are grown in planters or window boxes. However, there are a few points that can make all the difference between the plants

Perennial plants (*above*) should be
planted in John Innes Potting
Compost No 3. Soil-less composts
are not recommended except for
parsley, chives and mint (*below*)

merely existing and flourishing. A plant grown in a container directly reflects the quality of the compost in which it is growing and herbs are no exception. A good compost is a priority.

Some gardeners think that they can mix up a suitable compost themselves by taking garden soil, sand, peat and fertiliser, producing a concoction that looks good, but is nevertheless unsterilised and with unknown nutrient levels. Weed seed will germinate and weeds proliferate, together with all kinds of pathogens and slugs and snails. Such a compost, usually made on the grounds of economy, must be avoided at all costs. What is wanted is John Innes Potting Compost No3. This is made from sterilised loam, sand and peat with John Innes Base Fertiliser added in varying proportions according to the number. No3 is the strongest and longest lasting, being intended for perennial plants rather than those of annual duration. Having a loam base it is an excellent compost for longer term planting, for if necessary you can use a liquid feed without any fear of the compost structure deteriorating as eventually happens with the peat, and peat-and-sand-based soil-less types.

Soil-less composts are a poor substitute for the John Innes kinds. They are relatively short-lived in terms of nutrient levels – just see how bedding plants forge ahead in their trays and then stand still if not regularly fed – while without the soil component their structure deteriorates badly. Few herbs grow naturally in such a peaty organic medium, so unless plenty of grit is added many subjects like basil, anise and rosemary are likely to rot off. The only merit that can be claimed for soil-less compost when growing herbs is its lighter weight where window boxes are involved, and then it is wise to be very selective about the herbs that are grown. Parsley, chives and mint seem to enjoy soil-less compost, but other popular sorts like thyme and marjoram have mixed feelings about it.

One of the major problems with planters and window boxes is keeping them moist during warm summer weather, especially if you are out at work all day and there is nobody to keep an eye on them. Try introducing a soil additive such as perlite or arcillite. These work just as well when incorporated with standard composts at about a 25 per cent by volume ratio. Being inert they do not affect the acidity, alkalinity or nutrient content of the compost. What they do is to enable moisture to be absorbed when you are watering, the particles releasing it back into the soil as it dries out. This enables containers to be watered less frequently and overcomes to some extent the stress caused to a plant by alternate drying and dampening which can reduce its foliage quality considerably.

Apart from compost quality, the other major factor in successful container cultivation is drainage. It really cannot be stressed too much. A waterlogged container will be the end of your herb display. If you have an attractive container with no proper drainage hole, then it is necessary to put a generous layer of shingle or broken crocks in the bottom before introducing the compost. This is not really adequate, but it is better than nothing. As drainage material now occupies space that should be taken by compost, herbs can rarely be recommended for small or shallow containers.

MAINTAINING HERBS INDOORS

Almost as many cooks as gardeners have an interest in raising fresh herbs, and cooks are not always gardeners. Herbs grown in the house must receive the maximum amount of light possible, especially during the winter, although they must never be cooked by fierce sun through an unprotected window. During the summer they benefit from spending fine days out of doors in an open sunny spot. It is no use thinking that warmth will be a substitute for light. Temperature and light must be in compatible ratios. This is most difficult to get right during the winter and early spring when natural light values are poor and we raise the temperature of our homes to make life more comfortable. At this time it is wisest to put your herb collection in the coolest, lightest place possible. Even an unheated porch or sun lounge is better than the kitchen window sill for the mid-winter and early spring months. Getting the correct ratio between light and temperature is difficult to achieve and herbs are the finest indicators of when you have it wrong! If your plants are drawn and pale with wide distances between the leaf joints, then you are in trouble. When this happens, cut down all the unnatural foliage and move the plants to a better environment. Never persist with weedy, drawn foliage.

Composts are also important. Never be tempted to take a pot outside and scoop up some soil, however good you think it may be, in order to plant a herb indoors. That is rather like feeding a racehorse on mouldy grain and expecting him to win the Derby. A good sterilized medium with a correct balance of nutrients is vital for success. Of course there are many to choose from, but for the most consistent results select one of the John Innes potting composts. These are a soil-based mix and provide good stable growth. If feeding becomes necessary it will not destroy the structure of the compost as the soil provides a buffer.

For long term herbs like thyme, marjoram, and chives John Innes No3 Potting Compost should be used. Plants grown in this will continue happily in such a medium for eighteen months to two years without needing to be repotted, although towards the end of that time they may benefit from an occasional liquid feed such as that popularly used for houseplants. John Innes No2 Potting Compost is for plants that are likely to remain in the same pots for a period of a year, or eighteen months at the outside. It does not have such a high nutrient level as No3 and is suited to medium term herbs like parsley and chervil. Those of annual or ephemeral duration such as basil and dill can be grown in John Innes No1 Potting Compost. For most of them, up to 25 per cent by volume of sharp grit added to the compost gives them the drainage which they desire. If for any reason you have to use peat or peat-and-sand soil-less compost, the addition of a similar proportion by volume of sharp grit is essential. However, few herbs really prosper in such a medium and I am generally against its use for the growing on of pot herbs, although on occasions it can be used to advantage for seed sowing and the raising of young plants.

Repotting
Potting and repotting cause some consternation to the newcomer. While one of the simplest gardening operations, it is often surrounded by mystique. How do we know if a healthy established herb needs fresh compost and a larger pot? Well the easiest way to get to know, and unfortunately the most commonly followed method, is to leave plants until they begin to suffer stress. If foliage starts to look pale and the compost is a little stale, often with tiny flies jumping around on its surface, then even the most unsure know that something must be done. The plant will certainly recover, providing that you do not let this condition go on too long, but it is much better to catch it early so that lusty growth can continue unchecked.

During the active growing period do not be frightened to turn plants out of their pots and inspect the roots. There is no need to poke the rootball about, but a regular inspection will show you whether things are in good order. Roots naturally gravitate to the edge of the pot, so do not consider the mere presence of roots on the outside of the rootball as necessarily meaning that the plant needs repotting. Nor is it always an indication that the plant requires a larger pot if the roots poke out of the drainage holes. This more often than not

93

indicates that you are not watering your plants regularly enough and the roots have come out seeking water from the gravel or the saucer on which the pot is placed. This is very common amongst pot grown plants of any kind that are watered from the bottom, although with herbs this practice cannot be recommended as it does not give proper control over the watering. The same also applies for the most part to the modern self-watering systems for house plants.

So how do you tell if your plant needs repotting? Pinch the rootball with your fingers. If there is any give at all the compost is not fully ramified by the roots and therefore the plant can remain where it is. If when you pinch the rootball it is firm, get the plant repotted right away.

Both plastic and clay pots can be used for repotting, clay ones usually giving the best results. A greater measure of control can be exercised over the moisture content of the compost in clay pots, although perfectly acceptable plants can be grown in plastic pots and bowls. The only proviso is that they have adequate drainage holes. All pots used in the home must have some kind of drainage, not just the gravel or crocks recommended for larger containers outside, but an escape route for excess water. When potting, ensure that the holes in the bottom of the pot are covered by a little gravel or broken plant pot. Then add sufficient compost to cover the drainage material. Remove the plant to be potted from its pot and if the rootball is very congested run a knife down it in two or three places to allow the roots to break out. If the pot ball is not tight and just nicely solid, then leave it undisturbed. The plant is centred in the new pot and compost is packed down with the fingers – never the thumbs as this gives uneven pressure – between the old rootball and the edge of the pot. There should be room to get your fingers down the side of the pot, and you should choose a new pot size that is two sizes larger than the old one.

Repotting. Always ensure adequate drainage, choose a new pot two sizes larger than the old one, and firm down the compost using fingers (not thumbs) to give an even pressure

95

Lightly top off the compost, allowing about 1cm (⅓in) from the top of the pot to the compost to give room to water. If you use John Innes Potting Compost, the compost must be firmed down before watering. If you use a soil-less kind, the compost is placed in the pot, the pot tapped to level off the surface, and the first watering will settle it down. Never pack soil-less compost tightly into a pot. Apart from excluding air it is difficult to wet thoroughly.

Potting-up

Potting up only differs in so far as the rooted cutting or seedling is going to be planted in its first pot. As it has no root ball and is in effect bare-rooted, great care has to be taken to see that a pot of sufficient size to accommodate the existing root system, and in keeping with the aerial parts of the plant, is chosen. One of the commonest errors when potting a young plant for the first time, is to put it into a large pot with the idea that it will not need potting so regularly. Only rarely does this work, for what in practice happens is that the large body of compost around the plant becomes wet and stale, the young roots encounter this and then struggle or die back. When placed in the pot, the plant should be held firmly and the compost gently poured around the roots. See that the plant is going to be at the same level in the pot as it was in the seed tray or propagator. Never firm the compost down, even if you are using the John Innes kind. It is much better to let the first watering settle it so that minimal damage is caused to the brittle young roots. After potting see that seedlings and cuttings receive adequate water, but remember that they do not yet have a rootball and the compost is vulnerable to waterlogging. Once active growth is witnessed then the plants have an established root system. If you regularly attend to repotting and ensure that light and warmth are in harmony, there are likely to be few problems.

96

When potting-up a new seedling, take care not to choose too large a pot. Hold the seedling in place and gently pour compost around the roots. Never firm the compost down, but let the first watering settle it to avoid damaging the brittle young roots

COPING WITH PROBLEMS

Fortunately there are relatively few pests and diseases that trouble herb plants. Some that are specific to one particular herb – mint rust for example – are dealt with in the text that follows the description of the herb in the A-Z. The problems that are outlined here are common to most herb plants at some time in their life. None are impossible to deal with, but as herbs are often used raw, directly from the plant, in cooking, any chemical cure has to be very carefully selected to prevent a health hazard.

Slugs and Snails

Of all the pests that attack herbs, slugs and snails are the most troublesome. These appear in many shapes, sizes and colours, but most feed upon the foliage, stems and roots of the plants. The large, evil-looking land-creeping slugs and snails are not difficult to control with modern slug pellets, especially those in which the active ingredient is methiocarb. Not only does this destroy slugs and snails, but leatherjackets, millipedes and woodlice as well. The more usual slug baits, both pellet and liquid, rely upon metaldehyde. While this is effective it is not as quick, clean and rapid as those which include methiocarb. Scatter the pellets among the succulent emerging shoots of established herbs during early spring. If you are worried about either birds or pets finding them, cover small groups of pellets, placed adjacent to the plants, with pieces of slate or tile raised slightly on stones so that the slugs and snails can gain access, but pets and birds cannot. Some gardeners recommend the use of beer placed in a small container such as an old margarine carton and sunk up to its rim in the ground. Snails and slugs find it irresistible and usually tumble in and drown.

Subterranean slugs, popularly known as keel slugs, are a different proposition as they live in the soil. They are very small, but have voracious appetites, devouring all manner of roots, ruining the crop and causing the plants to collapse. Liquid slug-killing formulations can be used to douse heavily infested soil with some effect, but the finest control is the exposure of soil to winter frosts. Apart from gaining some measure of control by chemical means, much can be done by maintaining a high level of garden hygiene. If attention is paid to the regular removal of dead or decaying foliage and weeds are kept under control, then little trouble should be experienced except on newly broken land where there is, quite naturally, a high level of infestation.

Greenfly

Greenfly are also a nuisance, especially on the shoots of established plants outside and young plants growing indoors in pots. Succulent leafy plants like basil are particularly vulnerable. In the early life of the plant a systemic insecticide can be used. Usually based upon dimethoate, this is absorbed by the plant into the sap stream and translocated throughout. Greenfly are sucking insects which pierce plant tissue and withdraw sap. When plants are regularly sprayed with a systemic insecticide the sap becomes lethal to the pest. With most formulations spraying is required every three weeks or so to give lasting protection. While this is quite satisfactory in the early life of a herb a high level of insecticide within the leaves is undesirable as harvest time approaches. About three weeks prior to cutting, switch your spraying routine to a weekly application of a pyrethrum-based product. This is a natural plant derivative which kills by contact. Harvesting is possible within a couple of days of the final application with no ill effects. Of all the insect pests, greenfly are the most debilitating, reproducing rapidly, stunting growth and destroying foliage quality. Plants that have been heavily infested with greenfly rarely produce any useable foliage.

Fungal disorders

The same applies if your herb plants suffer from fungal disorders like botrytis. This is not uncommon in damp seasons, causing discolouring and disfiguring of the foliage and sometimes dieback of leading growths. A number of fungal diseases, each producing similar symptoms, may occur, especially during wet summers. Positive identification of the malady is not vital, for a systemic fungicide based upon benomyl controls most fungal disorders. This behaves in a similar manner to a systemic insecticide, being translocated around the sap stream and providing protection. It should be applied before serious trouble develops. While it can arrest the spread of a fungal disorder, it is best applied as a preventative rather than a curative. Its use should finish about three weeks before harvesting, but, unlike insecticide, there is no safe alternative preharvest fungicide. So you just have to hope that the weather does not turn warm and humid during that period and encourage the appearance of fungal diseases.

Other insect pests and diseases will occasionally attack herb plants, but these are few and far between. In a well maintained garden where there is a high standard of hygiene few problems will occur. If your plants become afflicted by other pests and diseases, then act as you would if the herbs were part of the vegetable plot. No popular herbs are damaged by any commonly advocated chemical pest or disease control.

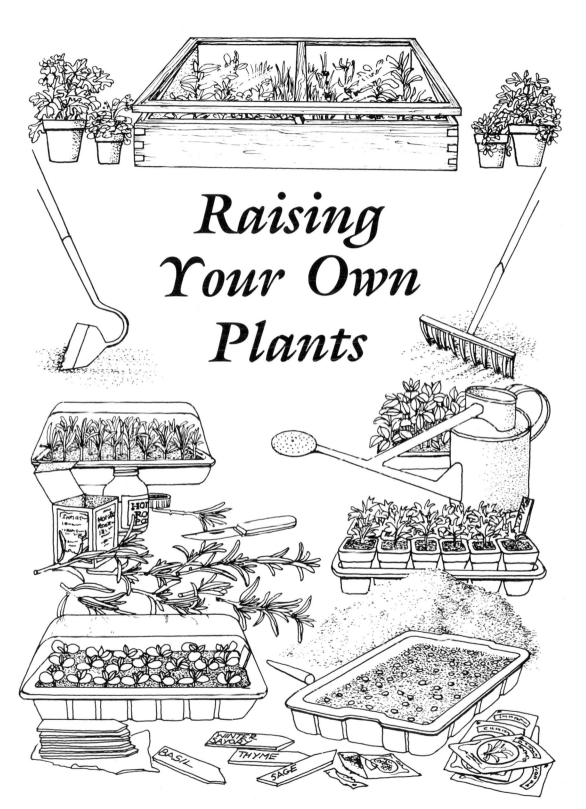

Raising Your Own Plants

RAISING your own plants is one of the most rewarding aspects of herb growing. You do not need sophisticated facilities for this as most of the varieties that we grow require only a sunny window ledge or small cold frame. If you have a small greenhouse or sun lounge, so much the better, for then even the more tricky ones like sweet basil can be grown with a reasonable amount of success.

RAISING HERBS FROM SEED INDOORS

Most popular herbs can be raised from seed sown with protection from March onwards. A few, like peppermint, benefit from a long season of growth and can be sown earlier if conditions are suitable. It is important with all species to ensure that at the time of sowing the ratio of heat to light is balanced, otherwise sickly, etiolated seedlings will be produced. If conditions are not suitable it is preferable to wait a couple of weeks until things improve. Although the resulting plants might not be quite as large, they will be healthier and better balanced. This problem is particularly acute when a window sill is used. The seedlings quickly germinate because of the warmth provided, but with the poor daylight that is inevitable in early spring, they become drawn and leggy. The ratio of light to temperature is so out of balance that the seedlings never make satisfactory progress.

Seeds being raised indoors should always be sown in trays or pans of good seed compost. As indicated earlier it is folly to go out into the garden and scoop up ordinary soil for seed raising. Even though such soil may look quite reasonable, it is likely to be of too poor a structure for use in trays and pans. Herb seed is full of vitality and has the main aim in life of germinating a healthy plant. It should not be hampered by poor compost. Apart from any other considerations, herb seed is not cheap, so do not be tempted to skimp in this respect. The plants that you raise will directly

Raising seed. **a** Fill the tray with chosen compost; **b** tap gently on the bench and firm corners and edges with fingers; **c** compost can be watered from above before sowing; **d** sprinkle seeds thinly and cover with about their own depth with compost; **e** water fine seed only from below by standing tray in water; **f** where no heat is available, place a sheet of newspaper over the tray to aid germination – remove as soon as shoots appear; **g** prick out when seed leaves are expanded and first true leaf is in evidence, holding seedling by the edge of the seed leaf; **h** bury seedling up to the level of seed leaves in new tray

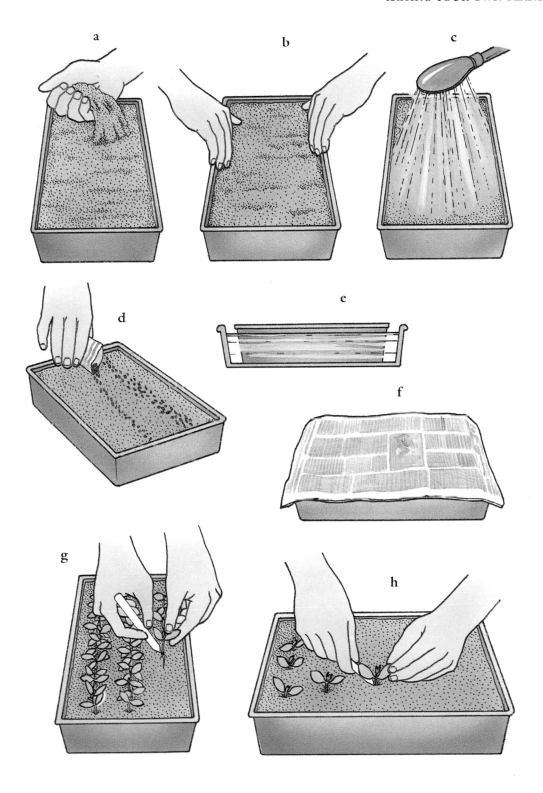

a

b

c

d

e

f

g

h

reflect the quality of the compost in which you are growing them.

Seed composts differ from potting composts in that they have few plant nutrients in them. The lack of fertiliser ensures that there is little likelihood of the tender seedlings being 'burned' and helps to dissuade troublesome mosses and liverworts which frequently invade the surface of seed pans. Soil-based composts of the John Innes formula are ideal for raising herbs, but certain of the quick-growing annual kinds ultimately make better plants if raised in a peat-based soil-less compost. Soil-less composts that consist of just peat, but with nutrients added, need handling carefully. It is necessary to be very selective about the kind of seed that you sow in them. Unless you can ensure a very smooth surface once the seed tray is filled, it is unwise to sow fine-seeded herbs like hyssop and peppermint in such composts. As it is so fibrous it creates air pockets in which tiny seeds can become stranded. Peat composts are ideal for larger-seeded plants like fennel and angelica. The smaller seeded herbs are much better in those soil-less composts which have sand mixed in with the peat. In any event, no matter what your preference, always seek a good branded kind. Unless you are going to enter commercial herb production, it is both cheaper and safer to purchase ready mixed compost rather than to try to formulate your own.

The pans or trays should be filled with seed compost to within 1cm (⅓in) of the rim. A soil-based compost should be firmed down before sowing, but the peat types merely need putting in a pan or tray, filling to the top and then tapping gently on the potting bench. This, together with the first watering, will firm the compost sufficiently. Firming down soil-less composts only succeeds in driving out the air and making them hostile to root development. It is essential with all composts to firm the corners and edges with the fingers when filling a seed tray. This counteracts any sinking around the edges and prevents the seed from being washed into the sides where it will germinate in a crowded mass. Seed compost can be watered from above prior to sowing. This is particularly useful with the soil-less types as it settles the compost and allows any surface irregularities to be rectified before sowing.

The seeds of most herbs can be sprinkled thinly over the compost and then covered by about their own depth. Large seeds like borage can be sown individually at regular intervals so that there is no need for pricking out. A light covering of compost is then dusted over. The majority of herb seeds need darkness in order to germinate satisfactorily. Some of the finer-seeded herbs are difficult to handle and distribute evenly over the surface of the compost. By mixing a little dry silver sand with the seed they can be more easily distributed. Not only does the sand serve as a carrier for the seed, but it also indicates the area of the compost over which the seed has been scattered. Fine seed should only be watered from beneath. Stand the tray in a bowl of water and allow the compost to dampen. Overhead watering can be disastrous, often redistributing the seed to the edge of the pan.

All herb seeds benefit from bottom heat, so where there is a soil-heating cable make full use of it. Warm compost promotes the rapid germination of most herb seeds and is particularly useful for gardeners who raise their plants in an unheated greenhouse. Where no heat is available a sheet of newspaper placed over a seed tray will act as insulation and creates a warmer micro-climate. Although light can penetrate the paper, it is important to remove it as soon as the seeds have germinated. With all seedlings light is vital so, as soon as they appear, place them where they can receive the maximum amount. This will ensure that they develop into stocky, short-jointed plants. Young seedlings of many herb plants, especially sage and rosemary, are very vulnerable to damping-off disease at this stage and watering should be carefully regulated. This unpleasant disease is prevalent in damp humid conditions, invading the stem tissues of the seedlings at soil level, causing them to blacken and the plant to collapse. Prevention is better than cure, so as a precaution water all emerging seedlings with Cheshunt Compound, a powder that can be mixed in the water and will ensure that the seedlings remain healthy.

All seedlings should be pricked out as soon as they are large enough to handle. Crowded seedlings are separated and individuals lifted and spaced out at regular intervals in pans or seed trays. Ideally seedlings should have their seed leaves fully expanded and the first true leaf in evidence before transplanting. Seedlings must be handled very carefully as they are delicate and often brittle. Never be tempted to hold a seedling by its root or stem as you can cause irreparable damage. Always hold it by the edge of the seed leaf. Rough handling at the pricking-out stage can lead to the spread of damping-off disease and the arrival of other pathogens. With most seedlings it is usual to plant them slightly lower in the compost than they were in the seed tray in which they germinated, generally burying the stem up to the level of the seed leaves. This should only be done to vigorous healthy seedlings. It is not a method of reducing the height of lanky seedlings that have been drawn up by insufficient light.

Seedlings must be pricked out in a potting compost. For most quick-growing herbs a standard soil-less potting mixture is adequate, but for the others John Innes No2 potting compost is preferable. Providing that there are no sharp temperature fluctuations and there is always plenty of light, the young plants should develop well. Apart from greenfly, few problems are likely to be encountered until the plants are either potted up individually or planted out. These pests are easily controlled with a systemic fungicide while the plants are young and you are not going to be using any of the foliage. There are now small aerosol cans available for handy use.

The most critical time for young herb plants is the period when they have to be eased away from their comfortable greenhouse or kitchen window-sill atmosphere and placed in a frame before facing the reality of the open garden. A cold frame is obviously ideal, for in bad weather the frame light, or top, can remain in place, whereas if the weather warms up it can be moved completely. The aim of this hardening-off process is to give the plants tolerance of the lower temperatures of the garden over a period of two or three weeks, without causing a check in their growth. When a frame is available the frame light is raised slightly to permit ventilation, gradually increasing until it is removed entirely during the day. It can then be raised at night to allow ventilation, gradually increasing until the frame light is removed entirely. The plants should then be ready to take their place in the herb garden. When a frame is not available, a similar effect can be achieved by taking the plants outside during the day and standing them in a sheltered place, returning them indoors each night until it is felt safe to leave them outside both day and night.

RAISING HERBS FROM SEED OUTSIDE
Some herbs dislike being transplanted even in their formative life and must therefore be sown directly into the open ground. Others are so easy to raise that the time expended in growing them in trays or pots is unnecessary. Good soil conditions are vital for direct sowings and these are brought about much more by correct autumn and winter cultivation than by those undertaken during the spring. A deeply dug soil which has been left to the mercy of the weather during the winter months is ideal. This should knock down with a hoe into a good friable soil that will provide perfect conditions for seed sowing. Spring dug soil will not be in such

good order, but, by incorporating a little sedge peat or the contents of old growing bags, the surface structure can be much improved.

Soil that has been well weathered should not be prepared until immediately before you are ready to sow. It may be tempting to knock the crumbling soil about a day or two in advance, but if it rains the soil will become compacted and the surface structure spoiled. It is important, however, that the soil is firmed before sowing. Shuffling your feet across the area after it has been knocked roughly level will be sufficient. A tilth can then be created with a rake. At this stage some gardeners like to mix a little fertiliser into the soil. While this may be quite satisfactory for vegetables and hardy annuals, it is not in my view desirable for the majority of herbs. As most derive from warm climates and impoverished soil, the addition of fertiliser, combined with our damp temperate weather, is unlikely to create favourable growing conditions. If a feed is thought desirable, it is better to use liquid fertiliser during the summer months.

In the southern part of Britain hardy herbs can be sown in the open ground from March onwards. In the north it is prudent to leave sowing until the end of April or early May. Do not be influenced by the date suggested on the seed packet, rather use your own judgement as to both soil and weather conditions. In some seasons it may be wiser to leave the sowing of certain subjects until early June, especially in more hostile northerly areas. Little is gained by sowing seeds in a cold, uncompromising clay soil. They are more likely to rot than germinate under such conditions.

If an area is to be devoted exclusively to seed-raised herbs, the positions of the groups can be marked out on the soil surface using a sprinkling of sand. A good visual effect can easily be achieved at this stage. While taller varieties are usually best towards the back of a planting, use some also towards the centre to avoid a regimented appearance. Also consider foliage colours and textures. Even with modest culinary herbs like mint, sage and fennel very attractive plantings can be created.

As with herb seeds that are sown inside, those going directly into open ground should be covered by about their own depth of soil. Some of the larger-seeded kinds, like angelica, can be sown individually, but most of the others will need to be broadcast evenly by hand over their designated area and raked in. Very fine-seeded kinds can be mixed with a little dry silver sand and scattered over the soil in a similar fashion to those being grown under glass.

It is vital that during dry weather newly sown seed and freshly emerged seedlings are regularly watered to ensure that their growth continues unchecked. Any seedlings that are crowded must be thinned as soon as they are large enough to handle or else they will become etiolated and subject to attack by the troublesome damping-off disease. In open ground the disease can cause considerable damage, whole colonies of seedlings succumbing in just a few days. Watering regularly with Cheshunt Compound will help prevent its occurrence. Rarely are any of the thinned seedlings any good for transplanting elsewhere. Those varieties that are readily transplantable are best raised with some protection anyway rather than in open ground.

RAISING HERBS FROM CUTTINGS

Many herbs can be increased from stem cuttings taken during the late spring and summer months. Shrubby subjects like hyssop, rosemary and thyme are readily propagated from non-flowering lateral shoots, although even shoots that are flowering can be rooted if the buds or blossoms are removed at the outset. It is important that cuttings are not hard and woody nor soft and flaccid. A semi-ripe cutting will still be green, but with a purplish or brownish cast. Having selected a suitable cutting

remove it from the parent plant with a sharp knife. Take away all the lower leaves that are likely to touch the rooting medium and cause decay. Apart from encouraging such problems these leaves will also continue to transpire, causing excessive moisture loss and wilting. A detached cutting must have balance between stem and foliage and often after the removal of lower leaves it is necessary to reduce the overall leaf area that remains. The stem should be cut at a node or leaf joint in order to expose the maximum concentration of active cells and thus enhance the chances of rooting. With larger cuttings, if the cut can be made at an angle an even greater potential rooting zone is exposed.

Both hormone rooting powders and liquids are invaluable aids to propagation as they encourage the development of root-forming cells and at the same time provide some protection from fungal diseases. Once the raw end of a cutting has been dipped in a hormone preparation it is ready for inserting in the rooting medium. Traditionally a mixture of equal parts by volume of sedge peat and sharp sand is used, but with the advent of materials like perlite and arcillite, which unquestionably give quicker and better results, the sand component is nowadays often replaced. Shallow seed trays are perfectly adequate for rooting cuttings, those that are placed towards the edge of the container tending to root more readily and quickly. Nobody is quite sure why this should be, but most practical gardeners acknowledge it as a fact. A moist atmosphere is desirable for all except the hairy-leafed kinds. A large kilner jar or plastic bag placed over each pan to retain moisture is ideal. Plants with hairy leaves will usually root quite readily in ordinary open-air conditions. Exposing them to a humid atmosphere will allow moisture to collect on the hairy leaves and encourage rotting. It is preferable to pot individual cuttings as soon as they root. Allowing them to become entangled in one another leads to losses when they are lifted as the

Sowing seed outdoors:
a Use a rake to create a fine tilth on well-prepared soil
b Mark the positions of the groups of plants by sprinkling sand
c Most herb seeds will need to be broadcast evenly by hand and raked in
d During dry weather, newly sown seed should be watered regularly

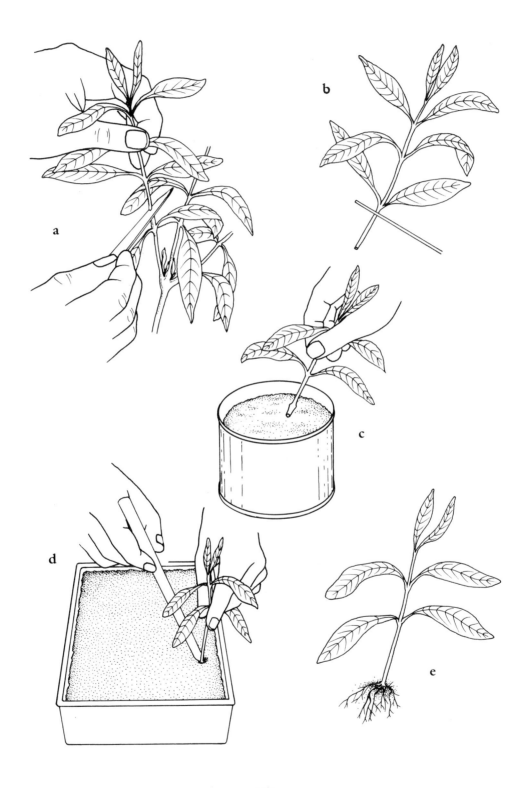

roots are extremely brittle and easily broken.

Apart from lateral stem cuttings as just des-cribed, a number of herbs, like lemon balm and marjoram, can be increased by short stem cuttings taken directly from the rootstock just as they push through the soil in spring. The shoots should be removed with a sharp knife at a leaf joint and treated in the same manner as a lateral stem cutting. Ensure that the stem of each cutting is solid. Hollow stemmed cuttings are difficult to root and should be discarded. Most herbs that can be treated in this manner root well under cold frame conditions.

Not only is it possible to take cuttings from the emerging shoots of herb plants, but in some cases this can be done from the roots as well. This applies to the artemisias which embrace popular subjects like tarragon and wormwood. Cuttings are taken during the dormant period, the adult plants being lifted and the roots exposed. Suitable cutting material is then removed and the parent plant replaced without any harm having been done. The best cuttings are made from roots that are full of the vigour of youth. They should be large enough to be able to survive without desiccating when replanted, and yet should never exceed the thick-ness of a pencil. Cuttings are made of pieces no more than 5 or 6cm long (2–2¼in) and these are placed horizontally in trays containing compost consisting of equal parts peat and sharp sand, although some gardeners prefer a little soil-based compost mixed in to give the medium a bit of body. The cuttings must be completely covered by the medium, well watered and then placed in a cold frame. The pieces of root should sprout the following spring and by early summer will be ready for potting or planting out.

DIVISION OF ROOTSTOCK

A number of herbs are readily increased by division of the rootstock during the winter. These include

Raising cuttings. **a** Remove a lateral shoot at a node or leaf joint, using a sharp knife; **b** remove lower leaves; **c** dip stem in hormone rooting powder; **d** place directly into rooting medium, towards the edge of the tray; **e** pot on as soon as cuttings have rooted

113

tansy, bergamot and lungwort. Indeed, many require regular division to maintain healthy vigorous stock. Carefully lift them with a fork and shake as much surplus soil off the roots as possible. This is easier in the autumn before the winter rains saturate the soil, especially on heavy land. To separate large clumps, insert two garden forks back to back and lever them apart. For most kinds it is usually only necessary to remove strong-growing offsets from the outer part of the clump. The less vigorous inner portion can be discarded.

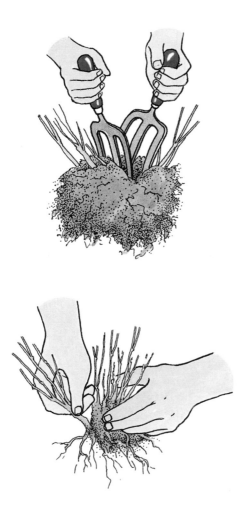

The Harvest

*T*HERE are no hard and fast rules about harvesting herbs, but there are a number of guidelines to follow to obtain the best results from your efforts. Fresh herbs can be picked when there are sufficient leaves or blossoms in evidence. Certainly fresh picked herbs are for the most part superior to those preserved in any way and full advantage should be taken of them when in season. For the most part the season is late spring through the summer, but those that provide a usable root are lifted between November and the end of February.

With many herbs it is either impossible or undesirable to pick and use them all at once and for these some method of preserving has to be undertaken. In the past herbs have always been dried, but freezing is increasingly becoming a successful alternative. In most cases it is not the method of preservation or storage that decrees whether the result is a success, it is the condition of the plant material when gathered.

GATHERING LEAVES

In order to obtain the best results, herbs must be gathered at the optimum time. This is when their volatile oil content is at its maximum, usually just before the plant comes into flower. You do have a little leeway with the harvesting time, for the oils are most evident from the time the flower buds start to form until they are partially open. However, there are exceptions. Parsley and chives, for example, can be cut at almost any time. It seems to make little difference with chives whether the flowers are present or not, but parsley, and to a lesser extent Russian tarragon, have foliage that becomes strong and unpleasant towards flowering time, so this is best gathered before the flower buds are seen. Fortunately, as parsley is a biennial, this is shortly before it expires. Sage should not be allowed to flower as leaf size and quality will be affected. With most herbs, however, it does not matter whether an odd partially opened flower or two is included when foliage is harvested.

It is preferable to gather herbs early in the day, for the oil content is highest prior to midday when the sun is at its peak. However, the foliage must always be dry when it is gathered so if it has rained, or there is still dew on the leaves, leave it until later. In the following section dealing with specific herbs I have mentioned any peculiarities regarding the harvesting of individual varieties. Fortunately most conform and the advice proffered here is fairly general for all.

Annual herbs are a category in which we are not concerned for the future of a growing plant. These are sown, grow, flower, and then expire all in one year, so we can cut these to within 10cm (4in) of the ground at the optimum time. Perennial herbs go on from year to year, so they have to be treated with more respect. If you wish to store a large quantity of a particular perennial herb, be bold and cut the plant to within about a third of its height from soil level. Most perennial herbs respond to this kind of treatment by throwing up another strong crop of foliage which can be harvested again in the same way. With a bit of luck a third cut will follow. Also, by regular cutting you get growth that is strong, healthy and full of the vigour of youth and far superior for preserving. Unfortunately this kind of production does not suit a herb garden that has to serve as a decorative feature too. If you are going to scalp your plants regularly they are best grown on the vegetable plot.

Never cut later than mid-September in the south of the country or the end of August in the north. Even if the herbs that you are growing have a reputation for toughness and hardiness they will still benefit from making a small recovery before winter weather creeps in. When cutting use a sharp knife. An old fashioned asparagus knife is the easiest to manipulate and of a good size. As the foliage is cut, spread it out gently in a trug or a box, taking care not to bruise the foliage. Never push

117

cut herbs into a bag, or leave them lying around in a heap, for within a very short time they will start to heat up very much like a compost heap.

Cut foliage needs to be picked over. Any stray weeds which have become entangled must be removed, together with occasional broken, yellowed or faded foliage, and any heavily mud-splattered basal leaves. If some of the leaves are dusty or slightly dirty, they can be rinsed with clear tepid water and gently shaken to remove surplus moisture before being spread out to dry off completely. Do not handle foliage excessively when preparing it for drying. Bruising the foliage releases the volatile oils which you are trying to preserve. Never gather more cut foliage than you can dry at any one given time. If left lying around untended, cut herbs deteriorate rapidly.

GATHERING FLOWERS
If you are gathering flowers, even greater care must be taken. They must be picked just as they open, and spread out on sheets of soft tissue paper in a tray or trug. Never pile them up, but spread them around so that they do not touch one another. Any that are showing signs of fading must not be gathered as they will already be losing their oils. Dirty flowers cannot be successfully washed so these also should not be picked. The aim is to harvest only whole, clean, unblemished flowers, especially if you intend to crystallise them.

GATHERING SEEDS
Seeds are a different proposition and probably the easiest portion of the plant to gather. Herbs commonly grown for seed, like fennel and dill are ready to use when they have turned brown. Unfortunately at that stage they are readily shed and even a slight breeze will cause them to dislodge, so keep an eye open for the development of the seeds and as soon as they turn yellow, cut the whole heads off with generous lengths of stem.

It is important when gathering herbs for drying that their volatile oil content is at its peak. This is during the period between bud formation and first flowering. They should ideally be gathered before the heat of the day

118

HERBS FOR DRYING

All these herbs are commonly dried
to ensure a year round supply.

HERBS	CUT FOR DRYING
Basil (Bush and Sweet)	Just before flowering.
Bay	All year round, but better during spring and early summer.
Borage	Whenever there are suitable young shoots.
Chervil	Summer, before flowering.
Chives	When leaves have attained full size.
Dill	Just before flowering.
Fennel	July until October.
Hyssop	As flowers appear. Both leaves and opening flowers can be dried.
Lemon Balm	June–September
Lovage	May–September
Marjoram (Sweet and Pot)	July–September
Mint (all varieties)	Just prior to flowering.
Parsley	June–July
Rosemary	June–August
Sage	June and August
Salad Burnet	When flower shoots appear.
Savory, Summer	When flowering.
Savory, Winter	Spring, as young shoots emerge.
Tarragon	June–September
Thyme	Before and at flowering time.

Invert the cut heads in brown paper bags such as greengrocers use and hang the bags from a string in a cool airy shed. The seeds will fall into the bag as they ripen and can then be dried and prepared for storage. Do not use polythene bags as condensation builds up inside and the seeds are likely to rot. Brown paper bags are quite absorbent, so you will rarely experience any mould problems providing that the seed heads are gathered when perfectly dry.

LIFTING ROOTS
Roots are harvested during the dormant winter season. Ideally they should be lifted just as the foliage dies back, for then they are plump and fresh. As winter progresses they start to deteriorate for they are preparing for growth. Horseradish, for example, can show signs of growth as early as February. Lift the roots carefully and brush the soil off thoroughly before drying.

With all herbs, the correct time for harvesting and the speed with which they can be processed will have a profound influence upon the product yielded. All should be kept out of the sun and removed to a cool place at the earliest opportunity.

DRYING HERBS
Growing herbs is one thing, drying them into the valuable green form is quite another. The skilful drier of herbs should be able to fool all but the gourmet that a dish garnished with dried herbs is seasoned with fresh foliage. The object when drying is to extract moisture but to retain as far as possible the original colour and oils of the plant.

It is not temperature alone that decrees whether the exercise is a success, free circulation of air is equally important. The moisture from the plant material must be carried away as quickly as possible by providing adequate ventilation. Ideally the herbs should be dried in the dark, as bright

121

sunlight causes deterioration of colour and evaporation of valuable oils.

In the past it was usual to hang bunches of herbs in a cool airy place and allow them to dry naturally. While this does yield quite satisfactory results with most herbs, drying them in the dark with a more controlled temperature and good ventilation leads to the greater retention of natural oils and a better colour. Commercially, herbs are dried with specially manufactured equipment and so the home gardener cannot expect such good results as seen in those little jars in the supermarket. However, you can come quite close by providing as near perfect conditions as possible.

Temperature is important, the ideal being some-where between 20 and 30°C. A lower temperature makes for very slow drying and a higher one, especially above 40°C, will ruin the foliage by drying it too rapidly. Good ventilation is also vital, the use of an electric fan being essential in a confined space. As the most suitable place for most gardeners to dry their herbs is likely to be an airing cupboard, such a contrivance is vital as the door must be kept closed to retain heat and maintain darkness. If no air circulation is provided, the foliage may well turn mouldy. Some gardeners use the oven set at a low temperature for drying herbs. While it is possible to achieve success this way, you are likely to ruin a considerable quantity of material before you get the process just right as each herb variety has a different optimum drying period.

Only with time and experience will you know when a herb has dried sufficiently. For the new-comer, the indication that a batch of herbs are ready for storage comes when the leaves are brittle to the touch and make a rustling sound when moved. If the leaves disintegrate, turning to flakes or powder, they have been overdone. So too has material which readily sheds its foliage. Stems and foliage should remain intact where both are to be used in the kitchen. Stems, if bent, should crack. If

CRYSTALLISED FLOWERS

A number of flowers of herbs and other plants can be successfully crystallised. Amongst these are borage, primrose, cowslip and violet. Most flowers can be treated in this way. Only those derived from bulbous plants are unsuitable as the majority are inedible.

Flowers are crystallised in a solution of gum arabic crystals and rose-flower water. Put 3tbsp rose water in a screw-top jar and add 3tbsp crystals. Leave for two or three days, shaking the jar occasionally until the mixture is viscous and rather like glue. The clean flowers that are to be crystallised should be spread out carefully on greaseproof paper and the sticky mixture applied to them with a soft, child's paint brush. The flowers should be 'painted' with the mixture, ensuring that all parts of the petal are covered. Any parts of the flower that are missed will quickly shrivel up. Dust the flowers lightly with caster sugar and then leave to dry, covering with a sheet of sugared greaseproof paper (made by coating the paper with egg white and dusting with caster sugar). The following day they can be stored in the dark.

they merely bend they are not sufficiently dry. Flowers that are being dried are ready when they no longer produce any stickiness, and fruits can be stored if, when rubbed together in the hands, they are sufficiently coarse and hard to make a scuffling noise. Roots need much more drying than foliage and can be considered ready when they are firm and brittle. If cut through they should not be soft in the centre.

STORING DRIED HERBS

Once satisfied that the herbs are sufficiently dried it is essential to get them into storage jars without delay. Leaving dried material lying around leads to its rapid deterioration. Not only is it likely to pick up moisture from the atmosphere, but most probably it will contract various moulds as well. Before removing dried herb material from the airing cupboard or the oven, have the storage containers ready. Ideally these should be airtight tins, although jars are perfectly adequate. Their only defect is that they let light fall upon the contents, although this is overcome if you store your herbs in a dark cupboard. Make sure that the jars or tins are clean and not tainted by the smell of previous contents. Metal containers, while being the best storage containers, can be harmful to the quality of dried material if it comes into direct contact with the metal, so either a small plastic container which will fit inside the metal one, or a lining of cardboard should be provided. To prevent tainting, ensure that only one herb type is assigned to each container. Storage of the tins or jars should ideally be in a cool dark cupboard.

FREEZING HERBS

As with most vegetables, herbs respond favourably to being deep frozen, especially those where the foliage is used. Although no extensive experimentation has been undertaken specifically with herbs, the methods commonly used for vegetables

HERBS FOR FREEZING

Most herbs can be frozen successfully, but some are not worth worrying about as fresh foliage is available for most of the year. These all freeze well and are seasonal.

Basil
(Sweet and Bush)
Chervil
Chives
Dill
(foliage)
Fennel

Lovage
Marjoram
(Sweet and Pot)
Mint
Parsley
Salad Burnet
Sorrel
Tarragon

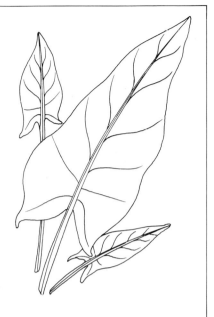

CANDIED ANGELICA

Candied angelica is invaluable for decorating and flavouring cakes, and the home-made variety has far more juice and flavour than bought angelica. April/early May is the best time to cut the young stems.

You will need:
Fresh young angelica stems, to make
  500g (1lb) after boiling
2.2 litres (4pt) brine made with
  8g (¼oz) salt
1kg (2lb) sugar
700ml (1pt) water
caster sugar

Method
Cut the angelica into short lengths no more than 10cm (4in) long and immerse them in the boiling brine. Leave to stand for 10 minutes, then drain. Rinse in cold water then boil in fresh water for about 7 minutes until tender. Drain again and scrape off the outer skins. Weigh.

Dissolve half the sugar in the water, bring to the boil and pour over the angelica. Leave for 24 hours. Drain off the syrup, add remaining sugar and bring back to the boil. Simmer for 5 minutes then pour over the angelica and leave for a further 24 hours.

Every day for the next 4 days at least, drain off the syrup, bring to the boil and simmer for 5 minutes, then pour back over the angelica.

Leave to soak for 2 weeks. Drain, then spread the angelica on greaseproof paper to dry slowly. When completely dry, roll the angelica in caster sugar and store in an airtight container.

have been quite satisfactory.

Ideally the herbs to be frozen are gathered in early morning with the dew still on them. They are shaken free of moisture and then placed in polythene bags, secured with a freezer tie and deep frozen. Some gardeners prefer to treat them in exactly the same way as vegetables and blanch the foliage before freezing. This involves immersing it in boiling water or steam for about one minute and then cooling it rapidly.

The exact method of blanching is not important. Usually the cut herbs are placed in a plastic colander – never use a metal one for herbs – and immersed in steam or boiling water. The same water can be used on several successive occasions providing that it is brought to the boil each time. After blanching shake the herbs vigorously to rid them of as much moisture as possible before packing in polythene bags in the usual manner ready for freezing. Unlike dried herbs, bulk storage is not practical as the contents would need thawing and re-freezing each time a pinch of herb is required. This would cause a rapid deterioration in quality. Deep-frozen herbs must be packaged in very small quantities so that what is needed is removed from the freezer at any one time. There is no need to label each tiny package, merely place all of one variety in a carton or large cardboard box and label that.

Bunches of freshly cut herbs should be hung in a cool airy place to dry before preparing for storage

A-Z
of
Herbs

The most popular garden herbs are listed in alphabetical order by common name. The Latin name follows, together with the family to which each herb belongs. Descriptions of each herb are followed by cultural routine and appropriate propagation techniques.

ACONITE

Aconitum napellus Ranunculaceae

This is not the tiny yellow-flowered winter aconite *Eranthis hyemalis*, but the plant known to gardeners as monkshood, the plant from which the highly dangerous drug aconite is extracted, a substance once used to tip poison arrows and bait wolf traps in years gone by. Today the extract is used as an anodyne, diuretic and diaphoretic.

Monkshood is a most attractive plant with dark green glossy foliage, not unlike that of a delphinium in general appearance, but with towering spikes of sinister, hooded, dark blue flowers. These are in evidence during late May and June, with a secondary flush from lateral shoots a couple of months later if dead-headed without delay. Adaptable as to soil and situation, *Aconitum napellus* prospers in all but the driest sun-baked position. Propagation can be from seed, but this takes at least two years to produce flowering-size plants. Alternatively the strong fibrous roots can be lifted and divided in the early spring, just as the bright green shoots push through the soil. Apart from the common species, there are several named cultivars of greater decorative value.

AGRIMONY

Agrimonia eupatoria Rosaceae

This is not widely cultivated now as its properties are called into question. It is also of doubtful garden merit, although, as it has a long tradition in old herb gardens and is well known to gardeners, it is often grown for sentimental reasons. Formerly valued as an ingredient of medicinal tea and a flavouring in beer, it is now only used as a dye plant. A useful yellow dye is obtained from the whole plant, although it is from the roots that it is most readily extracted. It has delicate yellow blossoms with a mild, sweet fragrance, clustered around slender flower stalks.

A hardy perennial, agrimony is easily increased by division during the winter, or seed sown where it is to grow during late summer or early spring. A native plant, it is easily grown in most soils and situations. Rarely growing more than 60cm (2ft) high, it is sometimes confused with the taller growing resin-scented *A.odorata*. This is of similar appearance but more frequently branched.

ALECOST

Tanacetum balsamita Compositae

A roguish plant, also called costmary, or mace, with pleasantly fragrant foliage formerly used as a strewing herb, its foliage has an attractive bluish bloom and in years gone by it was often used for bookmarks in church. This gave rise to the alternative name of bible leaf. Nowadays it is just a pleasant plant to have in the herb garden, although some enthusiasts encourage the regular production of fresh basal shoots by cutting the plant back frequently. These shoots are used in soups, stews and stuffings. As a medicinal herb it was once believed to be a reliable cure for catarrh and for strengthening the stomach, as well as providing flavouring for beer before hops were used.

When grown for its shoots it rarely ever flowers, for the plant is continually trimmed. This is no great loss, as the blossoms are paltry, rather like small yellow pom-pom chrysanthemums. A well-drained sunny site suits alecost well, its creeping roots spreading rapidly and colonising any vacant patch. It is by chopping up these creeping roots that the plant is most readily propagated, although it can be increased by short stem cuttings taken during early spring. These will root readily in a mixture of peat and perlite in about equal proportions and can be planted out the same summer. If the plants are going to be allowed to develop completely, plant them 45cm (18in) apart, but if constantly cut back it is more productive to close the distance to 30cm (1ft).

ALEXANDERS

Smyrnium olusatrum Umbelliferae

Although no longer grown for culinary purposes, this native herb is an interesting character with a long history of cultivation. Before celery was grown in Britain alexanders was favoured for its pungent celery-like flavour. Known by country people as horse parsley, this tall, ungainly perennial looks rather like a greenish-yellow cow parsley and is frequently encountered in coastal areas, especially in Scotland. Of little decorative merit, its inclusion in the herb garden is a matter of historical interest or nostalgia. It is easily propagated from seed sown where it is to flower and tolerates most soils and situations.

ALLSPICE

Calycanthus floridus Calycanthaceae

Both *Calycanthus floridus* and *C.macrophyllus* are referred to as allspice. *Calycanthus floridus* is Carolina allspice and *C.macrophyllus* Californian allspice. However, neither yield the allspice sold commercially, which is a flavouring derived from the dried, mature, but unripe berries of *Pimenta officinalis*, a relative of the common myrtle which grows in the balmier climate of the West Indies. Notwithstanding that, both *Calycanthus* are invaluable additions to the herb garden, by virtue of their fragrance and their shrubby habit which provides a backbone to the herb display. Both flower during August, *C.floridus* with purplish flowers and *C.macrophyllus* with blossoms of dark

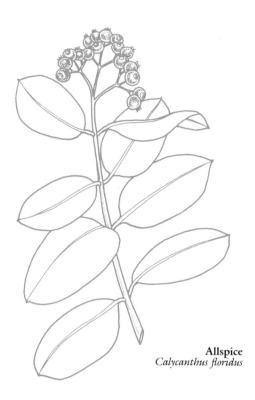

Allspice
Calycanthus floridus

ANGELICA
Angelica archangelica   Umbelliferae
This is a magnificent plant worth growing for its architectural qualities alone. Unfortunately it is usually only of biennial duration and therefore must be replaced annually if you want it to flower regularly in the herb garden. When given a cool moist soil in partial shade, however, this problem may not be apparent for it will seed itself freely and become almost 'perennial'. The seeds are of very short viability and best sown as soon as ripe. Seed that is kept until the spring rarely germinate freely and often not at all. Angelica also dislikes root disturbance and so seed must be sown where the plants are to grow, or else seedlings must be transferred to individual pots immediately they have germinated and grown on as pot plants until ready for planting out. When planting out allow plenty of room for development. Anything less than one metre between plants would be getting rather close.

A dignified plant some 2m (6ft) or more high, angelica has the general aspect of a quality cow parsley but with handsome segmented foliage and enormous domed heads of greenish-white flowers. These are very attractive to wasps and it is alleged that gardeners in years gone by have kept an eye on their angelica blossoms for the arrival of the queens. These find angelica irresistible and while indulging in its pleasures can be removed and destroyed. The stalks of angelica are candied for use in confectionery. They are also added to fruit dishes and jams as well as serving as a substitute for juniper berries in gin-making. It is possible to dry the leaves and stalks successfully if gathered before flowering, but ideally it is a herb which should be used fresh.

ANISE
Pimpinella anisum   Umbelliferae
This is a challenging plant to grow in most parts of Britain. Certainly in the north, on a cold uncompromising clay soil, it is unlikely to yield the round aromatic aniseed seeds for which it is grown. This is only reliable with cloche or frame cultivation. In the south of the country it is a very different proposition, producing an acceptable crop most years from the open garden. It is a delicate-leafed plant allied to angelica, dill and fennel, but much more temperamental. It adds little visually to the herb garden, and therefore should only be grown when a definite harvest is required.

Seed is sown in the open ground in April, being given the protection of a frame or cloches where possible. It requires a poor free-draining soil in full sun. One of the commonest causes of its demise is a rich soil which causes the plants to collapse and

red. The delightful allspice fragrance is produced by the leaves and wood of *C.floridus*, but *C.macrophyllus* depends upon richly fragrant flowers.

Allspice prefer a rich peaty soil in full sun. They are ideally planted during the dormant period, preferably from pots as bare-rooted plants rarely establish quickly. With modern container-growing techniques, calycanthus are generally available all the year around, but if you contemplate planting them in the summer months, be prepared to water them regularly. They need plenty of space as they can reach a height and width of 2m (6ft). Propagation is by seed when obtainable, this being sown in a frame and taking as long as a year to germinate. The most readily available method of propagation is layering and this can be done during July and August. Instead of pegging branches to the ground, it is better to peg them into a pot containing a good compost. Once rooted, the layer can be detached and the plant is then ready to grow on undisturbed in the pot.

rot at the base. Germination is usually quite rapid and even, however the seedlings have very fragile roots and rarely transplant successfully. Thin the seedlings once they have produced a few rough leaves, to about 20cm (8in) apart. The plants will attain a height of upwards of 60cm (2ft), but being rather thin and willowy they benefit from close planting. Cultivation presents few problems, although it would be unusual for all the seedlings to reach maturity. It is therefore prudent to remove any sickly plants the moment they are noticed. When the first umbels of seeds show signs of ripening, lift the entire plant and spread it out on newspaper in a warm place to dry out.

BASIL

Ocimum basilicum and ***O.minimum*** *Labiatae*
Both sweet basil, *Ocimum basilicum* and bush basil *O.minimum* are difficult to grow well, but are worth persevering with. Especially if you delight in the oriental tang of their foliage which is just perfect when used with tomatoes. Both are tender annuals and natives of India, with glossy green leaves on slender succulent stems. In the case of bush basil the leaves are quite small, rarely more than 1cm (½in) across and of a paler green than the larger-leafed sweet basil. Neither is a particularly large plant, bush basil rarely achieving more than 20cm (8in) and sweet basil little more than 30cm (1ft)

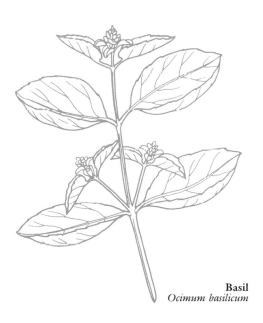

Basil
Ocimum basilicum

Sowing the seeds and raising the plants under glass or on the window sill is essential if the resulting plants are to get away quickly and not form hard woody stems. February is often suggested as being the time to sow seed, but most experienced gardeners agree that late March or early April is likely to give greater success. In fact sowing at monthly intervals during the summer is probably a good idea, for then succession can be achieved and drastic losses covered. It only takes a day with too high a temperature or too wet a compost for the plants to collapse.

Seed should be sown in a good seed compost and given the protection of a greenhouse or window sill, the temperature whenever possible being above 20°C to ensure a reasonably even germination. The tiny seedlings should not be touched until about 10cm (4in) high. If they have germinated reasonably evenly, they should come to no harm. Traditional pricking out and potting on can result in major losses without explanation while potting up larger plants causes fewer losses, even though the purists will tell you that this is bad practice. Be careful not to overpot, a 7.5cm (3in) pot is adequate to begin with.

BAY

Laurus nobilis *Lauraceae*
This is one of the best loved culinary herbal plants, the aromatic leaves being used either fresh or dried in stews, soups and sometimes fish dishes. The bay is the laurel of victors, the plant that we usually call laurel being a member of the *Prunus* or cherry family. It is a handsome evergreen shrub of doubtful hardiness in the north of England. Here in Yorkshire we usually treat it as a tub plant, providing indoor protection during winter. Even when planted in the open ground in more favoured locations it benefits from shelter, for searing winter winds burn the foliage, giving the plant an unsightly appearance and ruining the leafy harvest.

Bay trees are usually purchased in pots and can be planted at any time of the year. If they are being planted into the open garden, then it is better to get them in during spring so that they have the entire summer to become established. Watering is of course very important and protection from drying winds with a netting windbreak is essential during the first year. Bay prefers a free-draining soil, and when grown in a tub benefits from a soil-based compost like John Innes No3.

Propagation is by cuttings taken during the summer and placed in very close conditions in a propagator or a large pan over which a large jar is inverted to give the old-fashioned bell-jar effect. An equal parts by volume mixture of peat and

Bay
Laurus nobilis

perlite is the best rooting medium to use, but even with near perfect conditions success is likely to be very variable. Not only are the cuttings unpredictable in their ability to root, but also in the time it takes for root initiation. A wait of six months from inserting the cuttings until rooting is not unrealistic.

An alternative method of propagation is layering, which can be done during July or August, a low branch being pegged down at the tip. Rather than allowing it to root into the surrounding soil, it is better to provide a potful of a suitable rooting medium sunk into the ground and place the layer in this. Once it has rooted successfully it can be detached as a pot grown plant without any root disturbance.

BERGAMOT
Monarda didyma Labiatae
Bergamot is a popular herbaceous perennial from North America that is also known as bee balm or oswego tea, the latter name being derived from a beverage once commonly made from an infusion of its aromatic leaves. It is of little culinary value, but very pleasant to have around, not only for its oily scented foliage, but more especially for its vivid scarlet blossoms. These are arranged in a similar fashion to those of the common mint, to which bergamot is closely related. However, they

are many times larger and quite startling. In addition to the common red species there are also pink, white and purple flowered forms. Rarely growing more than 60cm (2ft) high, bergamot appreciates a little shade and a damp soil.

A creeping plant, bergamot can be readily increased by division of the rootstocks in early spring just as fresh growth is appearing. Alternatively short stem cuttings can be taken during late spring and early summer and rooted in a cold frame in a sandy medium. Grow the cuttings in pots until they have established a root ball and then plant them out in their permanent positions allowing about 30cm (1ft) between plants.

BISTORT
Polygonum bistorta Polygonaceae
No longer an important herb, the bistort is nevertheless an interesting addition to the herb garden. In times past the foliage of this relative of the sorrel was used as a vegetable and together with the nettle was an important constituent in Easter pudding. The roots have also been used during depressed times, dried and ground up into a flour. They are also an astringent and a source of the gallic and tannic acids formerly used in the tanning of leather. Of dock-like habit, this interesting creeping plant has erect, bright pink flower spikes and is a useful addition to the herbaceous border or wild garden.

A moisture-loving perennial, it can sometimes become a nuisance on heavy soils and a small enclosure may be necessary to restrict its exuberance. Propagation is by division of the roots during the winter or early spring. Plant small vigorous roots with a strong shoot at intervals of 10cm (8in) and these will soon knit together and form a tight colony.

BORAGE
Borago officinalis Boraginaceae
Borage is one of the most attractive plants for the herb garden. A tall coarse plant it attains a height of a metre or more and produces beautiful blue starry flowers with black centres. Although only biennial, borage seeds so freely that once you have a plant in your herb garden it is self-perpetuating. It prefers a moisture-retentive soil, often becoming dwarf and lean-looking in dry inhospitable conditions. The fresh young leaves are gathered and used in salads, having a taste akin to cucumber.

Some gardeners recommend drying the leaves for use out of season, suggesting that this is done at flowering time. While it is a commercially viable proposition, it is not possible for the home gardener as the leaves are rather succulent and turn black before drying. In addition to the foliage, the flowers are often utilised in fruit cups.

Borage should be sown during the spring where it is intended to remain. Sow thinly, as almost every seed germinates. Healthy vigorous plants need to be at least 30cm (1ft) apart. Crowded seedlings must be thinned, never transplanted. Even if they survive, they run straight to flower and produce only a minimum of useable foliage. As long as borage has sufficient moisture it will prosper, producing flowers at varying times during the summer and dying afterwards. Seed can be sown deliberately to replace the adult plants, but sufficient is usually shed naturally to ensure the plants' survival. Late sowings often produce plants in early autumn that do not have an opportunity to flower before the winter. These develop a tough basal rosette of foliage and usually pass through the winter unscathed. In addition to being a useful and decorative herb, borage is one of the finest plants for attracting bees.

CALAMINT

Calamintha officinalis Labiatae

The fashion for calamint tea has long passed by, but calamint is still an interesting and easy-going plant for the herb garden, sporting delicate sprays of mauve blossoms amongst low-growing downy foliage. Rarely exceeding 30cm (1ft) in height it is an excellent ground cover subject, flourishing in most situations, but preferring soil of an alkaline persuasion. Although it is easily increased from seed, it is usually so easily divided that it can more readily be propagated this way. Lift and divide the plants as soon as they start into growth during early spring.

Borage
Borago officinalis

CAPER SPURGE

Euphorbia lathyrus Euphorbiaceae

Traditionally grown by gardeners as a mole deterrent, but not to my knowledge having ever been proved successful, this interesting former medicinal herb has a rigid architectural quality about it that makes it an invaluable decorative plant for the herb garden. Its handsome glaucous foliage is arranged in a stiff angular fashion and topped by tiny flowers with yellowish-green bracts. It is these flowers that give way to the strange caper-like fruits to which the plant name alludes. These 'capers' should not be eaten, for like the majority of euphorbias all parts of the plant are acrid and most are poisonous too.

Caper spurge generally flourishes better on heavier soil. When in a situation to its liking it seeds freely and then becomes almost perennial, although it is technically an annual.

Seeds can be sown where they are to remain during early summer. It is possible to transplant seedlings, but take great care in handling them as if even slightly damaged they will exude a white latex material. This is an irritant, particularly if it comes into contact with the eyes, or skin abrasions. Although the mature spurge may grow up to a metre high it does not have a spreading habit. Seedlings can be thinned to as little as 25cm (10in) apart.

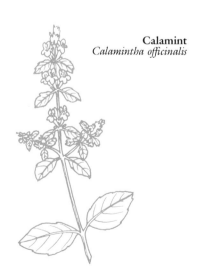

Calamint
Calamintha officinalis

CARAWAY
Carum carvi Umbelliferae

Caraway is an elegant biennial herb not unlike a small version of common fennel but with darker green foliage. It is the seeds for which the plant is commonly cultivated, these being used in confectionery and cakes. Plants raised from seed sown in the open garden during April flower in May the following year and yield seeds in July. The umbels of fruits do not all ripen at the same time and so it is best to cut the plants down as soon as the first show signs of ripening. These must be hung up in a dry, well ventilated place. To save losses the heads should be enclosed in brown paper bags. The seeds will then be captured by the bag if the fruits break open.

Caraway benefits from a fairly hungry, free-draining soil which must be in full sun. Although seedlings do not transplant well, it is vital that young plants are thinned out to at least 25cm (10in) apart.

Caraway
Carum carvi

CATMINT
Nepeta cataria Labiatae

The catmint of the old herbalist is not the catmint of the gardener. This is the native *Nepeta cataria*, a rather rank plant up to 1m (3ft) high with distinctive square stems and rough-cut, heart-shaped leaves. These have a greyish downy appearance and are surmounted by spikes of pale pinkish-white flowers. It was formerly used to make a tea before the importation of Indian tea. It was also used as a culinary herb, the foliage being rubbed onto meats before they were cooked. Nowadays it is grown more as a curio, especially by cat-lovers as cats love to roll in it, but the more decorative *N.mussini* and *N.nervosa* are of greater garden merit. It is the former that is widely cultivated as catmint, a handsome plant with billowing masses of greyish foliage and spires of mauve blossoms that are loved by bees. *Nepeta nervosa* is a more compact plant with green leaves and larger blue flowers.

All catmints demand a sunny situation if they are to prosper and, while tolerating most soils, will often die out during the winter on very heavy land. It is a wise precaution in any event to over-winter a few rooted cuttings. These can be taken at any time during the summer, from non-flowering material. They root very readily and can even be pushed individually into small pots of potting compost

Catmint
Nepeta cataria

with every expectation of them taking and growing on successfully. Just pinch the leading growths back when about 10cm (4in) high and a strong bushy plant will result. Nepeta can also be raised from seed sown in a tray of good compost during the spring. The young plants can be pricked out or potted individually into small pots. Seed sown during March will produce plants that can be planted out in June.

CELERY

Apium graveolens Umbelliferae

Celery is essentially a plant of the vegetable garden. However, it also figures quite prominently as a herb in flavouring dishes, especially those originating in North America, and so rightly finds a place here. Both dried and fresh foliage are used for seasoning, along with celery seed which is incorporated in soups. The foliage is reasonably easy to provide, but, within the confines of the ordinary garden, celery-seed production is not a sensible proposition. It is far better to purchase your seed requirements. Be cautious though, for seed sold for sowing in the garden is almost invariably dressed with thiram to control celery leaf spot and must on no account be eaten.

Celery is raised from seed sown under glass during February and March in just the same way as other herb or vegetable seedlings. It transplants easily and can be pricked out into trays ready for planting out after the danger of frost has passed, usually around the second week in June. Most gardeners grow their celery in trenches which can be flooded during dry periods. This also allows for soil to be drawn around the plants at a later date in order to blanch the stems. A well-prepared trench is essential and one that has plenty of well-rotted manure incorporated into the base during the winter is ideal. The trench should be of sufficient width to allow for the planting of two alternating rows of plants, 30cm (1ft) apart with 25cm (10in) between plants. The excavation should be carefully prepared, the walls sloping outwards so that they do not collapse when dried by the sun. The soil that has been removed should be placed in a long narrow, flattened bed on either side and this area used to grow a catch crop of lettuce before the soil is needed for blanching.

Earthing up begins during August, a little soil at a time being pushed into the trench until it is full and the stems are covered, or blanched. These days most gardeners blanch the lower part of the plant with soil, but enclose the upper portion in a paper or cardboard collar. When blanching celery, remove any suckers that sprout beside the plant and ensure that the collars are fitted in such a manner that rain trickles down the outside rather than into the heart. Celery can be left in the ground and dug as required, a good frosting improving the flavour.

There are many cultivars of celery available in both pink and white, although it is the white stemmed kinds that find most favour with cooks. The pink-stemmed sorts are merely offered with no other name than the ubiquitous 'Unrivalled' or 'Giant'. 'Giant White – Solid' is, however, a distinct cultivar and the one commonly grown by the traditional method. Others are mostly of the self-blanching type which eliminate the need for collars or earthing up. 'Golden Self-Blanching' is the common sort, a dwarf compact variety ideal for a confined space, while 'Lathom Blanching' is of greater stature.

Where the production of stems is not important, celery can be removed from the vegetable garden and mixed in with herbs. An informal group planted at about 25cm (10in) centres will form an attractive green stand of foliage. If it is the leaves that you are interested in, half a dozen plants will probably suffice. Pick the leaves before the frost arrives and dry any surplus. Although a biennial, celery rarely survives the winter intact and as a matter of course should be replaced annually.

CHAMOMILE

Anthemis nobilis Compositae

There are several plants which carry the name chamomile, but *Anthemis nobilis* is the one to which everyone refers when discussing herbs. More properly known now as *Chamaemelum nobile*, this lovely little plant has fine, green, lacy foliage and white daisy-like flowers with bright golden centres. The solitary flower heads were once dried and used medicinally as a tonic and febrifuge. However, it was more commonly used for chamomile lawns, especially on dry hostile soils where it would remain green for much longer than the majority of grass species. Nowadays it is generally grown as a pleasant aromatic plant which associates well with other herbs, although the arrival in recent years of a flowerless chamomile popularly called 'Treneague' has brought about a mini-revival in the chamomile lawn.

Ordinary *Anthemis nobilis* is easily raised from seed sown in situ during late March or April, or alternatively in a seed tray with the protection of a cold frame at about the same time. Raising plants in a frame is best when you have heavy soil, but is not necessary on lighter land. When raising seedlings in a tray prick them out as soon as they are large enough to handle, but instead of putting them in trays in the usual fashion, use the small modular peat trays that are divided into tiny individual pots. Young chamomile plants are floppy and difficult to handle unless grown in a pot from early on. Established plantlets can be put out as soon as they are able to withstand the rough and tumble of the garden, being planted about 10cm (4in) apart in each direction. Seedlings that have been raised from direct sown seed should be thinned to a similar distance.

Chamomile can be increased by division, or separation of small plantlets from the parent plant. This is best done during spring, the young plants being planted in their final positions. It is such plantlets that are used for creating a lawn, but here planting distances can be a little closer to speed up the rapid knitting together of the foliage. Prepare the site as for an ordinary lawn, ensuring a firm level surface and then carefully plant into this. For the first year it is vital to keep weeds under control which is quite a difficult task, as, unlike conventional lawns, selective herbicides cannot be used. So hand weeding is the order of the day and this will continue into the second year when a fairly complete cover should have been achieved. Unlike grass, chamomile lawns do not need regular cutting, although with ordinary *Anthemis nobilis* it is prudent to cut back flowering shoots as soon as they are noticed. Treneague chamomile is a different proposition and only requires stray or unruly shoots cutting out to keep it in good order.

Chamomile
Anthemis nobilis

CHERVIL
Anthriscus cerefolium Umbelliferae

Although widely cultivated in France and throughout Central Europe, this attractive and tasty parsley-like herb has never really caught on in this country. Usually treated as an annual, chervil also has the habits of a biennial subject, variable sowing periods rendering it unsure of which life cycle to follow.

An early sowing is the most satisfactory. Sow in pans of good seed compost during February or March, with frost-free protection. Chervil resents disturbance and benefits from being planted out from pots, so as soon as the seed germinates and the seedlings are large enough to handle, prick them out into small pots or tiny modular peat trays. Plant out in a free-draining soil in an open sunny situation about 10–15cm (4–6in) apart.

Where considerable quantities of chervil are needed, an early sowing can be made outside under cloches during March. Open-ground sowings made later than this usually run to seed before producing any appreciable quantity of usable foliage. Sowings made during August are more successful, yielding a leafy crop by late September and continuing into the winter with the protection of cloches. If not cut too severely during the early winter months, the plants will often recover and provide a couple of useful spring cuttings before they run to seed during early summer.

Chervil has an aniseed-like tang and when gathered fresh is used in much the same way as parsley, making delicious chervil soups and equally famous sauces. Whatever you use it for, it should be gathered directly from the plant and used straight away. It can be dried, but the trouble involved and the resultant poorer quality leaf make this a doubtful proposition, especially when it is so simple to ensure an almost year-round supply of fresh foliage.

CHICORY
Cichorium intybus Compositae

Although widely used by herbalists in the past, chicory is now considered to be more of a vegetable, the chicons being blanched and served as a salad. In the herb garden, where it can remain undisturbed, it provides an attractive splash of blue during summer when its shaggy dandelion-like blossoms appear. For salad purposes it is best grown in rows in the vegetable plot, the Witloof or Brussels chicory being the one to select.

Sow the seed sparingly in drills in the open ground during May and June, in rows 30cm (1ft) apart, thinning the emerging seedlings to 15cm (6in) apart. Keep them weed-free and well watered, removing any stray flower stems that

Chervil
Anthriscus cerefolium

Chicory
Cichorium intybus

appear. A fairly hungry soil is best, as one that has been recently manured produces forked roots that are inconvenient to force. When frost has turned the foliage yellow, the roots can be lifted and all the leafy remains removed. This is usually well into November and the roots should be prepared for forcing.

If you do not wish to force all the roots at once, those not being used can be heeled into a vacant corner of the garden. Select a few for the first crop and pack them tightly into a deep wooden box with peat or good clean garden soil. Place the box under the staging in the greenhouse, or in a dark cupboard. When utilising the space beneath the staging, exclude light by hanging a curtain of sacking across the front. If you can provide warm conditions, then the creamy-white chicons will be ready for cutting within a couple of weeks. Without heat they may well take a month or more. Once cut, secondary leafy growth will appear. Although this is edible it is of very poor quality, so dispense with the roots immediately the harvest has been gathered. During its period in the greenhouse it should not require any attention, the moisture in the peat or soil being sufficient to sustain life until harvest.

Apart from the popular Witloof chicory there is another kind which an adventurous herb grower should be prepared to try. This is Madgeburg chicory, the chicory of the coffee industry. It is from the roots of this plant that commercial coffee substitutes are procured, but in the garden so little is produced that it cannot be taken as a really serious proposition.

The plants can be grown in just the same way as ordinary forcing chicory, being lifted in the autumn at the same time. Once lifted, the roots should be dried, as much soil as possible removed from them, and then thoroughly scrubbed before being roasted in the oven. Once the roots have been roasted they can be ground down to produce a coffee substitute.

CHIVES

Allium schoenoprasum *Liliaceae*

Chives are an invaluable herb for the kitchen garden or window sill. Related to the onion, chives have thin onion-like leaves up to 15cm (6in) high and a swollen base that is not unlike a spring onion. The leaves are chopped and used for flavouring in salads, soups and stews, and the swollen bases can be diced and used like onions, although this does destroy the plant. Being hardy perennials, chives regenerate their slender green foliage regularly and can be cut throughout the summer months.

They usually flower during June and July, and

while the soft lilac-pink balls of flowers are a drain upon the plant's resources, they are very attractive and add a splash of colour to the herb border. Some gardeners consider it vital to remove the flowers. If you leave them until they just open and then cut them with as long a stem as possible, the flowers will retain their colour and can be dried for winter arrangements.

Chives grow in almost any soil in all but the shadiest of places, responding equally well to pot or window-box culture. They can be raised from seed sown during March in trays in a cold frame or on the window sill, or increased by division during early spring. Seed-raised plants are best treated like onions, the grassy seedlings being pricked out into trays as soon as they are large enough to handle. They can be potted individually into small pots, the compressed peat type being extremely useful. When grown in these the plants can be planted out complete with pots without suffering any disturbance. Plants from a March sowing are usually sufficiently robust to plant out towards the end of June or early July. Plant 15–20cm (6–8in) apart, either in a group or a long row.

Divisions are a much quicker way of producing plants for almost immediate cutting. While it is unwise to take foliage from seed-raised chives until late summer or early autumn, the leaves from

divisions can be cut much sooner. There is no difficulty with division, for when lifted a chives plant will naturally break into a number of segments, each not unlike a spring onion. Those selected for planting should have their tail-like roots trimmed hard back and then planted with the emerging shoots just beneath soil level. Although chives can be lifted and divided at any time during the dormant period, it is easier to separate and quickly re-establish them during early spring when the plants start into growth. Division is the only reliable method of increasing the so-called giant chives which are about half as big again as the ordinary species, with handsome foliage and bold, globular flower heads.

CLOVE CARNATION
Dianthus caryophyllus Caryophyllaceae
Clove carnations are no longer used herbally, although some people utilise them in perfumery. They are now simply good old-fashioned fragrant plants for the summer garden. Their use obviously extends well beyond the herb garden and into the herbaceous border, but it is amongst the elegant foliage and soft colours of herbs that these are best enjoyed, producing bold grey-green foliage and delicately sculptured blossoms of white, pink or red, rarely more than 40cm (16in) high.

Clove carnations are easily raised from cuttings or layering, the cuttings being taken in the same way as for garden pinks. Young shoots which have not flowered are selected and the cutting removed by holding the stem of the plant and giving a sharp tug. This pulls the cutting cleanly from what is virtually a socket and this can be rooted. This kind of cutting is called a piping and this method prevents the cutting falling to bits as is often the case when shoots are removed with a knife. The cutting should be rooted in a mixture of equal part by volume of peat and perlite, or peat and sharp sand. Rooted cuttings are best grown on in pots. As they must be taken during June and July, the resulting progeny are unlikely to be potted until towards the end of August and by this time it is getting rather late to plant them out. Overwinter in a cold frame and plant out the following March.

Layers need not be taken until July, trailing shoots being pegged down after an incision has been made at a leaf joint. It is wise to prepare pots of a suitable medium, sunk into the soil, and to peg the layers into these. A pot-grown plant then results. These too should be over-wintered in a cold frame. As carnations prefer an alkaline soil, it is useful to incorporate a little ground limestone into the soil prior to planting. Space the plants out at distances of between 25–40cm (10–16in) according to variety.

Clove Carnation
Dianthus caryophyllus

COLTSFOOT
Tussilago farfara *Compositae*

This native plant is much mistrusted by gardeners, largely because of its dandelion-like appearance. Of the same family, it rarely presents a serious problem unless you allow it to seed. The seeds are soft and silky, very much like the parachutes of the dandelion, and readily carried on the wind. In days gone by this was gathered and used for filling pillows.

I find the plant useful because of its early flowering period, short sturdy stems, supporting bright yellow daisy-like flowers appearing during February and early March. The leaves which follow are not especially attractive, being green with a greyish felt and roughly hoof-shaped, the feature which gave this plant its common name.

Previously used for all manner of medicinal purposes, coltsfoot is now only used in coltsfoot tea and in the manufacture of herbal tobacco. Old techniques of producing coltsfoot rock and coltsfoot syrup are now largely forgotten, although until recently the latter was listed in the *British Pharmacopoeia*.

Coltsfoot is a plant still locally abundant in the wild and seed gathered from such plants should germinate freely. It is also fast spreading by means

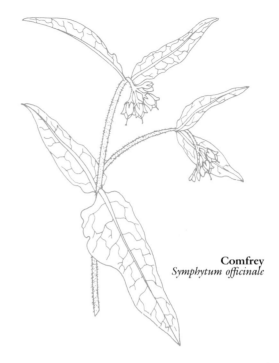

Comfrey
Symphytum officinale

of a creeping underground rootstock and small pieces of root lifted and removed at almost any season of the year will re-establish readily. Take care how you site coltsfoot in the herb border and where possible bury a shallow barrier to restrict its uncontrolled spread. It is indifferent as to soil, although it seems to prosper rather better on clay than in a light sandy medium, and providing that it is not in deep shade, will grow quite happily.

COMFREY
Symphytum officinale *Boraginaceae*

Much has been written during recent years about this rather coarse and rank native plant, with its large bristly leaves and hanging clusters of creamy-yellow or purplish flowers. Research into its properties has been undertaken recently by the Henry Doubleday Research Association, both as a food and medicinal plant as well as a fodder crop. Other research has been carried out into its value as an activator in compost heaps. So it would seem that the potential for this rather unassuming plant is considerable.

Traditionally both the roots and leaves of comfrey have been used medicinally. The root was prescribed for intestinal disorders, while the leaves were used for treating strains and bruises, as well as allegedly having the ability to unite broken bones. Thus, in certain parts of Britain, it is still referred

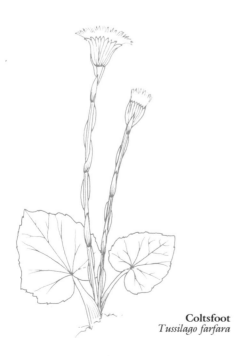

Coltsfoot
Tussilago farfara

to as knitbone. The colour of the flowers was also supposed to be significant, yellow- or creamy-flowered plants being used for treating women, while the darker purplish-flowered variety was used for men.

While no self-respecting gardener with a herb patch would leave comfrey out, it is a rather coarse, vulgar plant, best suited to the rear of the border where its charming pendant blossoms can be enjoyed, but its ugly leaves disguised by more elegant plants. It can also be a nuisance if not strictly controlled, so deal with any encroachment ruthlessly. This tendency to spread indicates that division is a ready means of propagation, although when lifting a plant it rarely falls into pieces of equal proportions. This is of little account, how-ever, as any healthy piece of root will take hold and produce a new plant.

If you are starting from scratch, comfrey can easily be raised from seed, although relatively few seedsmen seem to bother with it. Sow during March or April in a tray of John Innes Seed Compost. Providing that you are not heavy handed with the watering can, it will germinate freely and yield strong healthy young plants which can be planted out during the summer. As comfrey does not transplant readily when bare-rooted during the summer, it is more prudent to pot-grow the seedlings and then plant these out with as little disturbance as possible. Keep them very well watered and within two or three weeks they will become established.

Apart from very wet areas, comfrey will tolerate a wide range of soil conditions, although it tends to struggle a little on light soils, especially during hot sunny weather. Under these conditions it is wise to mulch the plants with well-rotted compost or animal manure before the weather turns warm and dry.

Apart from the true comfrey, there are a few other species that are worth considering. Although not having the same alleged properties as *Symphytum officinale*, the prickly comfrey, *S.asperum*, formerly grown for animal feed and sporting blue flowers, and our other native comfrey, *S.tuberosum*, with its smaller stature and creamy-yellow flowers, are both worthy additions to the herb collection. There is also a hybrid called *S.peregrinum*, and the blue comfrey, *S.caucasicum*, which are well worth acquiring. These are not infrequently encountered as garden escapes, for they were once grown as medicinal plants by farmers and smallholders as an alleged cure for foot-and-mouth disease in cattle. There is also an excellent ground-cover comfrey called *S.grandiflorum*, with pinkish-red flower buds which open creamy-yellow. Of neat, compact, low-growing habit, this is perhaps more at home amongst flowering shrubs in the mixed border, although there is no reason why its colourful blossoms should not be made full use of in the herb garden. All the comfrey species, like *S.officinale*, are readily propagated by division or root cuttings, and all enjoy similar growing con-ditions.

CORIANDER
Coriandrum sativum Umbelliferae

This amiable annual is grown for its 'seeds' which are used in flavourings. Attaining a height of up to 1m (3ft) coriander is easily grown in any free-draining soil in an open sunny situation. It is reminiscent of a small cow parsley, but with darker aromatic foliage and pinkish flowers. From an April sowing the fruits should be ready to harvest towards the end of August. As soon as they look ripe and the foliage takes on a jaded appearance, the plant should be uprooted, the fruiting heads inverted in large paper bags and the plants suspended from the roof of the garden shed. When the plants have turned crisp and light brown they can be threshed to extract the 'seeds'.

Coriander does not transplant very successfully, so is best sown where it is to mature. It is rather slow and unpredictable to germinate, so rather more seed than usual has to be sown to ensure a good stand of plants. Thin at the seedling stage to about 25cm (10in) apart in each direction. The plants grow lustily and need no support, pro-ducing their delicate pinkish blossoms in July.

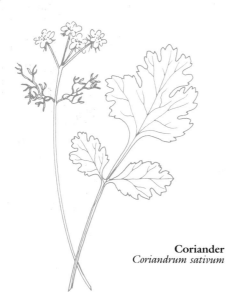

Coriander
Coriandrum sativum

COTTON LAVENDER
Santolina chamaecyparissus *Compositae*

Cotton lavender is one of the hardiest and loveliest grey-leafed plants for the British garden. Hardy in most parts of the country, it does sometimes succumb during the winter to cold, wet conditions, especially on heavy clay soil. However, it is so easily propagated that most gardeners regard it as a short-lived plant which benefits from regular replacement. Certainly that is how we grow it here at Harlow Car. Take short non-flowering stem cuttings during August and root these in an equal parts by volume mixture of peat and sharp sand in a frame. They root readily and can usually be potted up within a month. Use fairly small pots and a compost that is not going to encourage soft growth. John Innes Potting Compost No1 is ideal for, apart from not being over-endowed with plant nutrients, it is easier to control the moisture level during the winter months than is the case with soil-less composts. A cold frame will provide sufficient protection and the plants can be planted out the following April. Even if old plants have survived the winter, it is a much better proposition to start again as these often break into growth unevenly and lose foliage around the base, generally looking untidy and taking most of the summer to recover. Young vigorous plants always look good by July.

Being a southern European plant, cotton lavender enjoys a position in full sun. It also requires good drainage and produces its best foliage on a hungry soil. When planted on well-manured land, it tends to grow out of character with soft, lush foliage which, in a wet summer, will often develop botrytis. Apart from the popular species there are two other commonly grown kinds which benefit from identical treatment. The most attractive is *S.neapolitana*, often listed by nurserymen as *S.rosmarinifolia*, a grey-leafed type of very compact growth. Like the ordinary species, this rarely grows more than 45cm (18in) high. Neither does the green leafed *S.viridis*, a similar-looking plant with vivid green leaves that looks nothing on its own, but is a perfect foil for the other two. All have strange yellow or cream disc-like flowers which look like daisies, but without the petals.

Cotton lavender was formerly cultivated for its medicinal properties which included curing ringworm. The leaves were also dried and hung amongst clothes as a moth repellant. Nowadays it is grown primarily for its decorative value and sweet musky fragrance. Finding a place in the herb garden as well as the mixed border, cotton lavender can also be used to great effect as a low, informal hedge. With proper maintenance it can be used like lavender and indeed, in Tudor times,

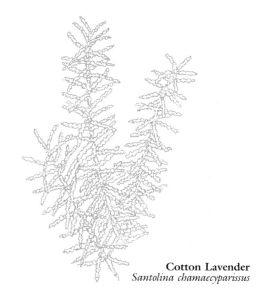

Cotton Lavender
Santolina chamaecyparissus

was treated quite severely when planted in formal knot gardens. To maintain a cotton lavender hedge in good order it needs clipping regularly from the time it breaks into growth during March. This does mean that the flowers are sacrificed, but most gardeners find them distracting when cotton lavender is also used as a hedge. If you do consider the possibilities of introducing a cotton lavender hedge into your garden, pay particular attention to the soil before planting. If you intend keeping a neat, clipped barrier, it is important that growth is regular and there are no wet pockets which could lead to individual plants dying off in the winter and creating unpleasant gaps. Good drainage before planting is vital.

CUMIN
Cuminum cyminum *Umbelliferae*

Cumin is a small half-hardy annual plant from North Africa which has largely been superseded by caraway. It has the same aroma but is nowhere near as productive. Although once a highly prized spice and reputedly a fore-runner of tobacco, it is now generally regarded as a charming and decorative plant and as an ingredient in Indian dishes. It is closely allied to cow parsley and fennel, with finely cut foliage and umbels of white or pink flowers.

Sow cumin where it is to flower, ideally in a well-drained soil in a sheltered position. An April sowing will yield a crop of fruits that are ready to harvest towards the end of August. Seedlings do not transplant well, so thinnings cannot be utilised. To create a pleasing effect the plants should be spaced no more than 15cm (6in) apart.

CURRY PLANT

Helichrysum angustifolium *Compositae*
This plant has nothing at all to do with curry, but has aromatic foliage with the same spicy fragrance. It is an attractive, shrubby, grey-leafed plant closely allied to the popular hanging-basket plant *Helichrysum petiolatum*. Like that species, the curry plant is also vulnerable to winter damage and as a precaution young plants should be overwintered. Take cuttings of non-flowered shoots during August, rooting them in an equal parts mixture of peat and perlite, or peat and sharp sand. The young rooted cuttings must be potted into a soil-based compost. John Innes Potting Compost No1 is the best as this has a relatively low level of nutrients and it is not desirable to promote soft growth before the winter. Overwintered in a cold frame, the plants can be put out again during April in a well-drained soil in an open sunny position. Even if old plants come through the winter unscathed, much better plants are produced from freshly planted young stock.

Curry Plant
Helichrysum angustifolium

DANDELION

Taraxacum officinale *Compositae*
Although one of the commonest and most troublesome weeds, the dandelion makes an interesting and tasty salad when cultivated. Selected forms under names such as 'Thick-leafed Improved' are the ones to choose and these should be sown during March and April in the open ground. Although quite amenable to cultivation in the herb garden, dandelions are more easily managed in the vegetable plot if you intend growing more than just a couple of plants. Here they can be sown in drills in the same way as carrots or radish. If more than one row is contemplated, ensure that the drills are at least 45cm (18in) apart.

Germination and growth are rapid on a well-cultivated soil rich in organic matter. Once the plants have reached 10cm (4in) high they must be thinned to 30cm (1ft) apart. The seedlings that are removed should be discarded as dandelion does not transplant satisfactorily under garden conditions. Allow growth to continue unchecked throughout the summer, just removing flower heads to prevent seeding and enable all the strength of the plant to be concentrated upon leaf production. If you gather the flower heads just as they open, they can be turned into dandelion wine.

In the autumn the rows can be earthed up, as advocated for celery, in order to blanch the leaves. Alternatively, the roots can all be lifted, trimmed, and then grown on in the same way as Witloof chicory, only the best leaves being selected for a salad. After blanching indoors, it is best to dry the roots out and then dispose of them on the bonfire. This will prevent any chance of them escaping and colonising other parts of the garden.

It is possible to blanch individual plants in the open ground by placing a large pot over the crown during the autumn. This gives the same effect as lifting and blanching indoors and has the advantage of being possible in the mixed herb border without disturbance. Providing that you do not blanch the same plant year after year, they can remain where they are. In the years between forcing, there is no reason why young succulent dandelion leaves should not be picked and used like lettuce in salad dishes.

DILL

Peucedanum graveolens *Umbelliferae*
An ungainly plant with a pungent, sharply aromatic flavour, dill cannot easily be mistaken for any other herb. Its delicate feathery foliage is used fresh in fish or egg dishes or with vegetables, while in Europe the seeds are ground and used in soups or salads. The seeds are also a source of medicinal oil. Although an annual, it is possible to grow at least two crops of dill a year, for dill matures very rapidly.

A direct sowing made in the open ground during March will yield fresh foliage for harvesting during early June, or seed towards the end of July. If fresh leaves are the main requirement, then successive sowings can be made until early June. Dill dislikes root disturbance and is unsuitable for transplanting. Attaining a height of around 60cm

(2ft) when flowering, it is a thin wiry character and can be grown as close as 15cm (6in) apart. Dill needs little attention, but benefits from a free-draining soil in an open sunny situation.

Leaves for garnishing can be gathered fresh, but when seeds are required it is best to wait until the lowest fruits on the stem are ripe and then carefully cut the plant down, shaking it as little as possible. The plants can then be dried out and the seeds shaken free. Dill seeds can be stored in airtight jars.

ELDER

Sambucus nigra *Sambucaceae*

The elder tree is a common inhabitant of the countryside and much loved by country folk for its many and varied properties, a number of which are still of value today. The creamy-white flowers produced during June and July have a strong odour and are used in wine making, for elder-flower pancakes and elderflower tea. The fruits, which are harvested during September and October, are also used for wine, jam, chutney and syrup as well as yielding a useful dye. All parts of the plant, including the roots, stems and wood have in the past been utilised for both medicinal and economic purposes, the leaves being once recommended as an insecticide. Gardeners used to take fresh shoots of elder, bruise them, and then gently beat their crops to ward off greenfly, while in some parts of the country it was traditional to plant elder trees around the outdoor privy to ward off flies.

In the garden the common species needs placing with care, for it is a rather untidy tree. However, it is easy to cultivate and succeeds on the most hostile soils. Rarely obtainable as a container-grown plant, the common species is usually purchased from open ground and transplanted in the dormant period. As a tree it is not particularly shapely and almost impossible to grow on a single trunk as a standard or half standard. Its natural habit is to make vigorous shrub-like growth, although in time this develops into sizeable branches. This must be tolerated and used to advantage wherever possible.

Unlike with most garden trees, when planting elder do not incorporate any good-quality planting mixture into the hole, but depend upon the existing soil. Rich soil conditions promote growth that is out of character. However, a proper hole should be prepared with the soil in the bottom broken up. It should also be of suitable dimensions to accommodate the root spread without diffi-culty.

Apart from the very useful common species, there are a number of decorative cultivars which,

to a greater or lesser extent, embrace most of the qualities offered by *Sambucus nigra*. These also require the same conditions and treatment as the ordinary kind, the emphasis on poorer soil being important for cultivars with strong foliage colours. Of these decorative kinds, one of the nicest is the golden elder, *S.nigra* 'Aurea', and the luxuriant butter-yellow leafed *S.n.* 'Plumosa Aurea'. Of the plain leafed kinds the cut-leafed elder, *S.nigra* 'Laciniata', is the most attractive, while the pink-tinted *S.n.var.rosea* 'Flore Pleno' is the most attractive of the flowering sorts.

Elder requires regular pruning to keep it within bounds, removing as much unproductive old wood as possible and encouraging new flowering shoots. In a traditional setting it is best to let the tree develop its own character and just seek to mould it. However, all the popular elders do respond to stooling, that is the regular removal of growth each spring almost to the base of the plant. This encourages basal shoots to develop rapidly, attaining 2m (6ft) at least each season. Not only is the growth vigorous, but the leaf size is often

Elder tree
Sambucus nigra

145

almost doubled, a particular bonus with the coloured-foliage cultivars. This cultural technique is very simple and enables most gardeners, irrespective of the size of plot, to have the opportunity of growing at least one cultivar.

If pruning is undertaken in February or early March, hardwood cuttings can be made out of suitable prunings. Do not skimp on material here. If you feel that the prunings are not of sufficient quality, discard them and start with specially selected cuttings. It takes several months to convert a bad shrubby specimen into a decent one, so care at the outset is essential. Short cuttings, about 15cm (6in) long, will root readily in a mixture of sand and peat in a cold frame, or alternatively in the traditional fashion, tied in bundles and pushed into the soil for half their length in a corner of the vegetable plot. With this method losses are likely to be greater, but at least half of the cuttings can be expected to root. When this has happened, it is preferable to grow the plants on a little in pots before planting them out in their permanent positions. A plant that has filled a 10cm (4in) pot is likely to be able to look after itself once planted out.

Elecampane
Inula helenium

ELECAMPANE
Inula helenium Compositae

This rather shaggy relative of the daisy is much loved by those who like the informality of the cottage garden, for this is a plant of that era, although it was cultivated by monks for centuries and is even suspected of being a native of the south of England. Nowadays it is grown purely for decoration, its previous virtues having been surpassed by modern science. Its most important use was in the production of cough mixture, its roots being a source of inulin. This also gave rise to its use in candies which were sucked to relieve asthma. Farmers often referred to elecampane as scabwort because of its alleged properties in healing sheep scab and townsfolk thought it an anodyne for the foul air that was given off by their open sewers.

In the herb border it is an attractive plant, a little over 1m (3ft) high with rather coarse dark green leaves and loose heads of interesting, shaggy, orange or yellow daisy-like flowers which, on fading, reveal velvety, brown seed heads. These can be dried for indoor decoration if cut in time. It is easily raised from seed sown in a pan of good seed compost either during the summer or in early spring. Most gardeners prefer a June or July sowing as this is not such a hectic time in the garden, the plants being of sufficient size to flower during the next summer. A spring sowing yields plants that may produce an odd spindly flower stem during the first year. Either way the seedlings benefit initially from the protection of a frame and are best grown on in pots until of sufficient size to be safely planted in the open.

Elecampane is also amenable to division, established clumps of plants being lifted during the winter months and split into individual crowns. The hardy woody central portions should be discarded, the smaller outer portions being replanted. These are full of vigour and ultimately make much better plants. Large woody pieces suggest rapid establishment, but in practice this is not so. Elecampane is an easy going and amiable plant that will grow happily in all but the driest soils and shadiest situations.

FENNEL
Foeniculum vulgare Umbelliferae

This is the perennial fennel, a handsome and striking plant up to 2m (6ft) high when in flower. It has delicate green filigree foliage possessed of the sweetest aniseed fragrance. Most herb growers recommend it for use in fish dishes or traditional fennel tea, but it is increasingly used now as a raw and tasty ingredient in salads. While it is possible to grow fennel from divisions of existing clumps, this is rather hazardous and some portions always fail. It is a much better proposition to raise young plants from seed. This can be sown in the open in April if the soil is in good order, the resulting seedlings being thinned out to 45cm (18in) apart.

Alternatively seed can be sown in a pan of good seed compost with the protection of a cold frame, or on the kitchen window sill during spring or early summer. As soon as the seedlings emerge, they must be pricked out into small peat pots, for fennel resents disturbance during later life. If pot-grown in a good soil-less potting compost, quite acceptable plants can be produced from an April sowing for planting out during July. These again should be allowed no less than 45cm (18in) between each plant.

Although fennel is a perennial, it is only usefully a short-lived one. After two or three years the centre of the plant becomes hard and woody and the surrounding growths diminish in size and quality. For those compelled to grow herbs in a mixed border, there is a purplish-leafed form of fennel, affectionately referred to as bronze fennel, which has greater visual attributes but similar culinary ones. While either will grow well on most soils, they prefer a moist free draining medium, especially in full sun.

FENNEL, SWEET
Foeniculum dulce *Umbelliferae*

This is a complete contrast to the popular perennial fennel, but one with which it is often confused. Also known as finnochio or Florence fennel, sweet fennel is rather more of a vegetable than a herb, although it can equally well be accommodated in the mixed herb border. It is a striking plant, of annual duration, with typical fennel-like foliage and swollen leaf bases that look somewhat bulbous and are blanched in much the same way as celery for use in winter salads.

If grown as a vegetable for its swollen leaf bases rather than for the foliage, it is best accommodated on the vegetable patch. Seed should be sown in April or May in drills 60cm (2ft) apart with the plants thinned at the first rough leaf stage to 20cm (8in). Sweet fennel does not transplant well and so the seedlings that are removed should be discarded, especially as their smell can serve as a lure for the troublesome carrot fly. Select a sheltered sunny spot, for Florence fennel needs a long warm season if it is going to give of its best. Earthing up of the swollen leaf bases should begin when they are a little larger than a golf ball, and this should carefully continue until the leaf bases reach maturity, at which time they ought to be more or less covered with soil and successfully blanched.

In British gardens this fennel has usually been regarded as a lost cause. Early importations of seed were not far removed from the ordinary species and did not prosper in the cool British summers. In recent years, however, some excellent cultivars have become available that will tolerate our unpredictable summers and produce good quality leaf bases which do not require as much earthing up in order to blanch them. A trial conducted at Harlow Car Gardens has shown that the most promising recent introduction is the cultivar called 'Perfection'.

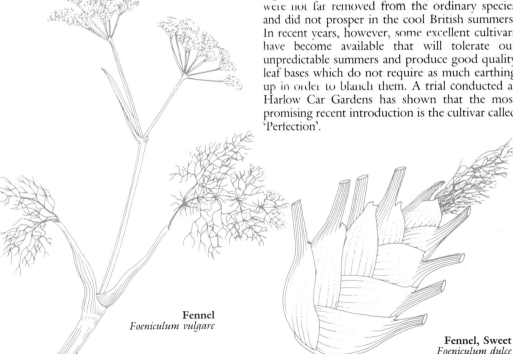

Fennel
Foeniculum vulgare

Fennel, Sweet
Foeniculum dulce

Feverfew
Chrysanthemum parthenium

FEVERFEW

Chrysanthemum parthenium Compositae

This is an interesting perennial herb with strongly scented pale green foliage and small white chrysanthemum-like flowers which appear during July and August. Seldom more than 75cm (30in) high, this rather ungainly, much-branched herb is currently being studied by serious medical bodies as a cure for migraine. Not that this is a new theory, for country folk have recognised its curative properties for many years. As a decorative plant it is somewhat unwieldy and its flowers are not especially beautiful. Indeed, when it is being cultivated for its foliage, the flowers are removed in the bud stage. So when cultivated in the herb patch, feverfew needs careful placing amongst other herbs if it is to blend in quietly. Apart from the ordinary species, there is a short-growing golden-foliage form called *var.aureum*. This is the popular 'Golden Feather' of the bedding-plant producer and is widely cultivated for formal and carpet bedding as a foliage plant.

Feverfew is easily raised from seed sown during March in a good seed compost in pans and placed in a cold frame. Although hardy, it does benefit from a little warmth in the early stages of development, so starting the seedlings off on the window sill is ideal. Once pricked out into trays, the plants can be gradually hardened off before planting in the open ground towards the end of May or early June. Most soils and situations are suitable, although extremes of dryness or dampness are not tolerated, nor heavy shade.

FLAX

Linum usitatissimum Linaceae

The uses to which this plant is put are legion and include linen production and the manufacture of linseed oil. While its uses are largely restricted to industry, and therefore it is not a productive plant in the herb garden, it is certainly a very decorative one. Indeed, it is probably the most charming of all herbs with delicate, narrow grey-green leaves and beautiful blue, or occasionally white, saucer-shaped flowers. A hardy perennial, its elegant appearance gives no hint of its resilience as a garden plant. Flourishing in all but the wettest soils, it prefers a sunny situation, but it will tolerate dappled shade. In gardens it is the straight species that is usually represented, although recently Harlow Car Gardens imported some seeds of named cultivars from the Latvian Academy of Sciences in Riga. These arrived with Russian common names which, upon translation, revealed attractive titles like 'Cobbler's Thread' and 'Spinner'. Showing marked improvements in both stature and quality, these cultivars are now being bulked up at Harlow Car ready for distribution to the horticultural trade.

Flax is very easily raised from seed sown with a

Flax
Linum usitatissimum

little protection in early spring. Sow in pans of a good soil-less compost and prick out the seedlings as soon as they are large enough to handle. Once well established in a tray, transfer the plants to small pots. If possible, do this before their wiry fibrous roots become too entangled. By the end of June quite acceptable plants will have been produced for planting in the open. When planting out, leave the rootball intact as flax dislikes disturbance when it has reached plantable size. It will flower the first summer, giving an increasingly impressive show for two or three years. It is then best replaced with fresh young plants.

In addition to ordinary flax, there is a species known as mountain flax, *L.catharticum*, an occasionally grown annual with delicate foliage and small white flowers. Not a particularly enthralling addition to the herb garden, it is easy going in most soils in an open position and yields foliage which is used as a purgative or made into a tea which is said to relieve rheumatism.

FOXGLOVE

Digitalis purpurea Scrophulariaceae

Our native foxglove is an important medicinal plant which provides digitalis, the active ingredient for certain heart stimulants.

In the garden it is a decorative plant which mixes and associates well with other herb plants. Of biennial duration, the common foxglove seeds itself freely and then becomes in all but name a perennial. Under the favourable conditions of moist acid soil and partial shade, its tall spires of pinkish-purple blossoms will attain a height of 2m (6ft), although under harsher circumstances it may well grow to no more than half that height. The leaves are broad, somewhat felty and a grey-green colour. Even during the period when not in flower the foliage of the foxglove lends character to a border.

Seed can be sown in situ in a well-prepared seed bed, the seedlings being transplanted when they reach the first rough leaf stage. Allow no more than 45cm (18in) between plants to obtain the best effect. Seed sown during the spring will produce lusty plants by the autumn and these will flower the following summer.

GARLIC

Allium sativum Liliaceae

This is too well known to need much description. A member of the onion family, it yields valuable oil and cloves or bulbils which are widely used for flavouring in continental cooking. In Britain this herb has strong associations with France and Italy and many gardeners believe that it is a southern European crop and therefore unsuited to outdoor

culture in this country. While it is true that it requires a good summer to produce a top quality crop, perfectly acceptable results can be obtained in all but the coolest and wettest British summer.

Garlic is another of the herbs best grown in the vegetable garden if you are seeking a sizeable, usable crop, but if you are growing it merely for interest, with the object of lifting a few cloves at the end of the season, it can be comfortably accommodated in the mixed herb bed. It benefits from a free-draining soil in an open sunny situation, the bulbs being divided up into cloves or bulbils and planted out during February or early March. If you obtain your stock from a nurseryman or seedsman, you are likely to pay rather a lot for it. The best way of obtaining stock is to visit your local greengrocer towards the end of January or early February. In all probability he will have a few clusters of garlic cloves left which by now are showing signs of sprouting and are becoming unsaleable. It is likely to be a good commercial selection or strain, and I have found that most greengrocers will accept a very reasonable offer to clear their stock.

In all respects garlic is cultivated like shallots, the cloves being planted out in rows 40cm (16in) apart with 15cm (6in) between plants. The area in which they are to be planted should have been well cultivated the winter before and allowed to settle. A light cultivation before planting, followed by an even firming of the bed, by shuffling on foot lightly across from side to side, will provide the best conditions. Routine care merely involves regular weeding. The foliage should die down of its own accord during mid to late August and, when of a light straw colour, the bulbs can be lifted. Spread them out in a dry place, preferably on a piece of wire netting raised off the ground so that air can circulate. Once any clinging soil has dried, this can be rubbed off and the garlic stored in a small net in a cool dry place. Only store firm bulbs. Any that show signs of damage or decay should be removed. Not only is the rot likely to be spread to the rest of the net bag, but it only takes a single bulb to decompose and become wet and soggy to induce the others to start sprouting.

GOOD KING HENRY

Chenopodium bonus-henricus Chenopodiaceae

This common native plant has been used as a medicinal herb, but was eaten more often as a vegetable in much the same way as spinach. Rarely is it grown nowadays for its large, more or less arrow-shaped leaves have a somewhat acrid tang and are much inferior to spinach. However, it is a very hardy perennial plant of easy disposition which is a good standby on the vegetable plot and an interesting addition to the herb border. Rarely growing more than 60cm (2ft) high, it produces rather uninspiring greenish flowers in compact spikes, so it is not a plant for the front of the border.

If you plan on growing this in the herb border, then just scatter a pinch of seed around in a vacant pocket. It will germinate freely if sown during March or early April and by July you will be able to pull leaves. It does not transplant too readily, so thinnings should be discarded, the remaining plants being left about 30cm (1ft) apart. In the vegetable garden it is sometimes treated with a little more care, the seedlings being raised under glass from a February sowing and then pricked out into small pots before being planted. This ensures an early crop of foliage, but is really unnecessary. Sowings can equally well be made in the open in shallow drills during March and early April.

Hemp Agrimony
Eupatorium cannabinum

HEMP AGRIMONY
Eupatorium cannabinum Compositae
Although no longer in use as a medicinal herb, hemp agrimony is an interesting plant to grow, especially in the wild garden. It has no startling decorative merit, being rather coarse with large billowing trusses of pinkish-mauve flowers. Nevertheless, this and its cousin, the North American Joe Pye Weed, *E.purpureum*, are worth cultivating and associate well with other herb plants, providing a dull green foil and, in the case of *E.purpureum*, colourful purple blossoms as well. This particular plant was highly respected amongst the Red Indians for its curative properties, its common name being derived from that of a well-respected medicine man. Apart from these two amiable characters there is another eupatorium that is occasionally grown, the boneset, *E.perfoliatum*. Unlike its cousins, this has white fluffy flowers.

Easy-going in any damp soil, all three much prefer dappled shade but will tolerate an open position if it is not too dry. They set seed freely, but this is not a reliable means of propagation. By dividing the roots during the dormant season, much better results can be obtained. Alternatively basal cuttings can be made from shoots as they emerge during early spring. These are easily rooted in a pan containing a mixture of equal parts by volume of peat and sharp sand, either in a frame or on the kitchen window sill. Take short-jointed cuttings about 5cm (2in) long and dip them in hormone rooting powder before inserting into the rooting medium. The cuttings will root quite quickly and can then be potted up into any good potting compost. Afford a little protection until late spring and plant out after hardening off, allowing 45–60cm (18–24in) between plants.

HOREHOUND
Marrubium vulgare Labiatae
When gardeners talk about horehound they usually mean the white horehound of the herbalist, not the unpleasant smelling black horehound, *Ballota nigra subsp. foetida*. The only virtue that this was said to have was as a curative for poison, although it was known in ancient times as mad-weed and thought to be an antidote to rabies. This is not a particularly useful plant for the herb garden. If you want to grow a horehound then use the pretty marrubium, an old-fashioned medicinal herb that was also widely used in the preparation of refreshing drinks, especially in East Anglia where it is still plentiful in the countryside. A short plant, between 30 and 45cm (12–18in) tall, it has undulating grey-green hairy leaves and pretty white axillary flowers.

Horehound
Marrubium vulgare

Horehound is a fairly reliable perennial, except on really heavy soil where in very wet winters it sometimes succumbs. It can be increased by short stem cuttings taken at any time during late spring when young shoots are looking strong and healthy. These root readily in a mixture of peat and sharp sand in a pan on the window sill, the young plants being potted up into John Innes Potting Compost No1 rather than a peat-based soil-less compost. Seed can be sown during March or April and will yield similar-sized plants by late summer. Use John Innes Seed Compost and give the same kind of protection as for cuttings. The seedlings emerge quickly and should be pricked out as soon as they are large enough to handle, eventually being transferred to small pots until large enough to plant in the garden. It is also possible to divide the roots of horehound carefully during the spring, replanting them in a free-draining soil in an open sunny position.

HORSERADISH

Cochlearia armoracia Cruciferae
Horseradish is one of the easiest herbs to grow, but one that needs careful placing if it is not to become a nuisance. Although most people recognise its fleshy roots – the main constituent of horseradish sauce – few are familiar with its large, coarse, dock-like leaves and spindly heads of white flowers. An unappealing plant visually, it is best grown in a quiet corner of the garden where it will not offend the eye, nor interfere with its neighbours. The commonly advocated method of curbing its exuberance is to confine it to a bottomless bucket buried in the soil. Unfortunately, while the plant will survive such treatment and not spread significantly, it is unlikely to yield good-quality roots. If a physical constraint is to be employed, then build a special sunken enclosure made of something substantial, like bricks or concrete blocks cemented together. Fill this excavation with good rich soil and a quality harvest will be assured.

The roots or thongs of horseradish are planted during the winter as soon as the soil is in a workable condition. Short cuttings of root are used, pieces up to 15cm (6in) long and at least as thick as a pencil being dibbled into holes 30cm (1ft) deep and as much apart. The holes should be filled with fine compost or sifted soil and the plants allowed to grow naturally. Apart from keeping weeds under control, little attention is required, for horseradish suffers from few pests and diseases.

The roots are lifted during the autumn after the leaves have been frosted and have died down. The whole crop can be lifted and stored in boxes of sand, although for most households it is sufficient to lift roots as required. Apart from being the main component of horseradish sauce, it has in the past been used medicinally as a stimulant, diuretic, antiseptic and laxative.

Horseradish
Cochlearia armoracia

HYSSOP
Hyssopus officinalis Labiatae
Hyssop is one of the nicest herbs for the small garden, being colourful, fragrant and well behaved, and also lending itself to garden, pot or window-box cultivation. A dwarf shrubby plant up to 45cm (18in) tall, it is cultivated for its leaves which have been widely used medicinally, and also for the making of hyssop tea, the optimum time for gathering foliage being as the lovely spires of blue flowers are opening, generally between July and September. Apart from the ordinary blue-flowered kind, there is a splendid dwarf species popularly known as the rock hyssop, *Hyssopus aristatus*. In every respect a dwarf version of the ordinary hyssop, this has the added virtue of being able to be grown in a pocket in the rock garden. Apart from their herbal and decorative merits, all the hyssops display a shrubby habit which lends itself to clipping as a low hedge. Indeed, like both cotton lavender and lavender, hyssop can provide an added bonus within the garden as a low internal hedge, or else as a neat evergreen edging to the herb bed.

Hyssop is easily raised from seed sown in a good seed compost in pans on the window sill or in the cold frame. It germinates freely if sown during March or April without artificial heat. As soon as the seedlings are large enough to handle comfortably, they should be pricked out into John Innes Potting Compost No1. Once of sufficient size to live happily in a small pot they must be moved on. Never get into the position of planting out young hyssop plants directly from a seed tray. That is a

Hyssop
Hyssopus officinalis

recipe for failure. Hyssop should always be planted out from pots or cultivated in them on the window sill. Seedlings raised from a March sowing are ready to plant out during June and will probably produce a few flowers by late summer. The following year they will be in full production. Ensure that they have a warm sunny position in a free-draining soil and they will prosper. In an informal setting the foliage can be cut as required, but, when used as a low hedge, it is best to trim during March when the worst of the winter weather has passed.

Cuttings of hyssop can be taken during the growing season. This is especially useful if a seed-raised batch of plants has given rise to a particularly good-coloured flower form. Any non-flowering shoots, about 5cm (2in) long, which are removed at a leaf joint will root readily. Use either a mixture of equal parts peat and sharp sand or peat and perlite as a rooting medium and you are almost guaranteed success. However, once potted, the young plants benefit from the protection of a cold frame for the first winter, being planted in their permanent quarters around the middle of March.

JUNIPER
Juniperus communis Cupressaceae
This is one of our three native conifers, the others being the Scots pine and the yew. It is a rather untidy plant that is difficult to keep in order in the garden, but should not be neglected, for it is one of the few evergreen inhabitants of the herb garden. It is cultivated for its 'berries', strange little fruits that are the source of oil of juniper and used in the production of gin. They take quite a period to ripen, so both mature amd immature berries will be found on the same plant, but not in vast quantities, so the inclusion of juniper in the garden scene must be purely for its visual effect.

Fortunately juniper grows on a wide range of soils and in most situations except dense shade. It is an amiable plant that can be kept within bounds by regular pruning each August. Never leave it until it has got out of hand before trimming it back, as rarely does a juniper break out properly into fresh green growth when wood more than two years old is cut into. It is also inconsistent in shape and size, occurring as a flat-topped shrub or pyramidal conifer, and everything between, depending upon which part of the British Isles it originated from. In commercial garden centres it is the more conical shape that is likely to be encountered, a fairly neat habit which, if unrestricted, will reach three or 4m high (13ft) and half as much through.

Junipers are easily raised from seed if you know

how. The seed, which usually comes to hand as dried berries, suffers from a condition popularly known as double dormancy, in which it usually needs the effect of two winters before it will germinate. So you can either allow the seeds to spend two winters outside in their pans in a cold frame, or alternatively they can be sown, and then subjected to two winters in the deep freeze! In both cases John Innes Seed Compost should be used. Being soil-based this is much more suitable for seeds that are going to take a long time to germinate as it does not lose its structure as readily as soil-less composts.

Sow the seeds in a pan and water thoroughly. If you are going to provide the seeds with an artificial winter they can be sown at almost any time. If you are going to rely upon natural methods, then an early autumn sowing is adequate. In this case the pan should be placed outside in a frame with the frame light removed and allowed to take all that nature can throw at it. If you are not patient enough to let nature take its course, place the pan of seeds (not the seeds in their packet) in the freezer and leave it there for two or three weeks. The pan can then be removed and subjected to room temperature for about six weeks. This replaces summer and then winter can be applied again by returning the pan to the freezer for another two or three weeks. Once removed and left in a warm light place germination should occur. This may not be rapid, very little appearing for at least a month, and it will also be erratic, so the pan must be left for at least a further six months to make sure that everything that is going to come up has adequate opportunity. Once the seedlings are large enough to handle, they must be potted into tiny pots using John Innes Potting Compost No1.

Junipers can also be increased by cuttings. These are taken during September and October, or else March and April. From all points of view the early autumn is the best, the cuttings being able to root without the risk of drying out or shrivelling up in hot sunny weather. Short lateral shoots are selected and removed with a heel. This is a piece of the old wood and cuttings can be easily detached from the plant together with this if given a sharp tug. When removing juniper cuttings, never use a knife and do not bother to utilise any terminal growths, even if they look suitable. Once you have gathered sufficient cuttings, trim up the heel of old wood with a knife and dip the cut ends into a hormone rooting powder. Use a mixture of either equal parts peat and sharp sand or peat and perlite in a pan or deep tray. Take far more cuttings than you need as juniper is not easy to root and, even with ideal conditions, cuttings taken during September or October are unlikely to be rooted and ready to pot until the spring. Pot them in John Innes Potting Compost No1, taking care not to damage the very fragile wiry roots. Grow the young plants on in pots as they dislike root disturbance. Whether grown from seed, cuttings, or purchased, it is always wise to plant junipers that have been pot grown rather than open-ground specimens.

Apart from our native juniper there is another species that is also used by herbalists, *Juniperus sabina*, a pleasant little species from which fresh foliage is gathered and dried to produce savin which is employed in medicinal ointments. In every respect cultivation and propagation are the same as for the common *J.communis*.

Juniper
Juniperus communis

Lady's Mantle
Alchemilla vulgaris

LADY'S MANTLE
Alchemilla mollis, A.vulgaris Rosaceae

The lady's mantle of the herbalist is the native *Alchemilla vulgaris*, but that of the gardener is the more showy *A.mollis*. Both are lovely hardy herbaceous perennials with green fan-shaped leaves with scalloped edges that are supposed to resemble a mantle. The soft green leaves are velvety and catch the dew or rain drops which run about just like quicksilver. The flowers of all alchemillas are rather mundane, being pale lime green, extremely small, and borne on elegant stems in dense corymbs. Both alchemillas are decorative, but where this is the main concern, choose *A.mollis* as it is a much more substantial plant. If you are considering using lady's mantle in the traditional manner, as a medicinal herb or to fill a herbal pillow, then you should really grow the more untidy *A.vulgaris*.

Lady's mantle is easily raised from seed. Indeed, once established, if precautions are not taken, self-seeding will cause problems. The removal of fading flower heads will keep self-perpetuation under control. Initially, though, raising plants from seed is the most satisfactory way as the woody root-stocks of alchemillas do not divide readily. Seed can be sown in the place where the plants are to grow, crowded seedlings being thinned to about 30cm (1ft) apart in each direction, the seedlings thus removed being utilised elsewhere. A spring sowing will often produce plants that raise an odd flower stem the same summer.

Apart from the two popular kinds, there is a short-growing species called *A.alpina* which is less than half the size, but of the same general aspect. There is also the plant known as parsley break-stone, *A.arvensis*, which allegedly cured gall stones. This is an annual, rarely more than 10cm (4in) high, with similar, but stalkless, greenish flowers, which enjoys an open situation on a light gravelly soil.

LAVENDER
Lavandula angustifolia Labiatae

This is the old English lavender, also known botanically as *Lavandula officinalis* and *L.spica*. Too well known to need much description, lavender is amongst the most popular of British garden plants with a diversity of uses that extends from the herb garden to the mixed border and the low formal hedge. Nowadays there are innumerable cultivars available for different purposes and the species themselves are so muddled and inbred that when choosing what purports to be straightforward old English lavender you really need to see the plant to make sure it is what you expect.

Cultivars are a different proposition as they are propagated vegetatively and are uniform and true to type. Apart from traditional lavender of the *L.angustifolia* type, there is a white-flowered form called 'Alba', a broad-leafed cultivar called 'Grappenhall' and a pink-flowered kind called 'Loddon Pink'. Each is of similar habit and stature and when flowering attains a height of 1m (3ft) or more. 'Hidcote' and 'Munstead' head the list of dwarf cultivars suitable for hedging. These are typical of their larger cousins in every respect, with bold spikes of lavender-blue blossoms, but they rarely grow more than 60cm (2ft) high. 'Twickel Purple' is another good compact kind, a dark-flowered compliment to the paler 'Folgate'. All flower during late June and July, prospering on almost any well-drained soil, but demanding an open sunny position. They are all perfectly hardy in most parts of Britain, although they occasionally lose some foliage in severe winters. The French lavender, *L.stoechas*, is not so hardy and in Yorkshire we keep this in a cold greenhouse for the winter. It is worth this trouble for it is a neat compact plant with intensely aromatic foliage and dense spikes of dark purple flowers. Most gardeners grow lavender for its delightful combination of fragrance, colour and form which make it a most versatile, decorative garden plant. However, some people make lavender bags for placing in drawers and wardrobes amongst clothes, these popularly being produced from the freshly cut flower spikes, although foliage can be included too.

All the cultivars of lavender, with the exception of 'Munstead', must be increased from cuttings.

These can be taken at any time during the summer months, from non-flowering shoots. While it is relatively easy to root cuttings of the current season's growth, it is better to remove them with a piece of the old wood. Tear the shoot away allowing a heel to remain attached. These will root readily in a mixture of equal parts peat and sand or peat and perlite if given the protection of a frame or window sill. Once rooted, pot the young plants individually, using John Innes Compost No2. Avoid soiless composts as these cause damping-off problems with young lavender plants if you are not extremely careful with the watering. The plants are best overwintered in a cold frame and then planted out in the spring.

All lavenders can be raised quite easily from a spring sowing using John Innes Seed Compost and utilising a frame. Even the cultivar 'Munstead' is successful from seed, producing plants of surprising uniformity. Sow during March and April, potting the seedlings up as soon as they are large enough to handle and treating them in the same manner as advocated for cuttings. Propagation of lavenders should form a regular part of herb-garden maintenance and renewal, for although lavender bushes will live for many years, they soon become woody and unsightly. To some extent this can be prevented by regularly cutting back in the spring and encouraging fresh growth, but there is a limit as to how often you can do this effectively, so I would advocate the replacement of lavender bushes every five or six years.

Lavender
Lavandula angustifolia

LEMON BALM
Melissa officinalis Labiatae

If you like the sharp fragrance of citrus, then this is the herb for you. It is the finest lemon-scented plant capable of cultivation outdoors in the British Isles. Of nettle-like appearance, this hardy perennial plant is also of value as a bee plant, the tiny white flowers, produced amongst the foliage in mid-summer, being alive with bees. Such is the reputation of this plant amongst bee-keepers, that it was once customary to rub its foliage around the entrances to beehives to ensure that the bees returned home. Its more practical use nowadays is in the preparation of lemon drinks and perfumes, and as a source of lemon flavouring in cooking. Try lining a dish with fresh foliage before preparing a lemon meringue pie.

The ordinary herb is plain green, but there are golden and variegated forms. The golden one is charming, especially during early spring when its foliage first appears. This is a rich butter yellow, but, with the passage of time, fades to lime green. The variegated form is not so attractive, even though it is quite startling. The yellow variegation is not consistent and tends to appear as irregular blotches rather than a proper variegation.

All three forms are easily propagated from cuttings of basal growth taken during April or May, just as the plant is coming into growth. Select strong short-jointed shoots no more than 5 or 6cm (2 2¼in) long and insert them in a mixture of peat and sand or peat and perlite. Given the protection of a frame or window sill, rooting will be rapid and by August they will have grown to sufficient size to be planted out. Pot culture from the rooted cutting stage is vital, as lemon balm resents disturbance during the growing season. It is also possible to lift and divide existing clumps, but unless strong healthy young growth is selected, the plants will be mediocre. It is best to select healthy young pieces of plant in early spring just as they are coming into leaf and then pot these up. In three or four weeks they will have become established in the pots and a month or so later can be planted out as good vigorous pot-grown plants.

The ordinary species can be grown easily from seed sown during March either with the protection of a frame or window sill. Use a good seed compost and sow sparingly as the seed germinates freely. Prick out into trays as soon as the first rough leaves appear and then move on into pots. While in the early stages of growth the compost that is used seems of little account, but the best adult plants are produced when they are grown on in a John Innes Potting Compost, the No1 formulation yielding stocky plants that become well established.

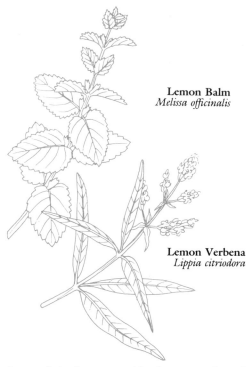

Lemon Balm
Melissa officinalis

Lemon Verbena
Lippia citriodora

Lemon balm is an amenable plant on moist soils and in the majority of situations. However, it is not always reliably winter-hardy in the north, so treat it rather like hardy fuchsias. Leave the old stems and foliage intact to protect the crowns during the winter, removing them towards the end of March when the first basal shoots appear. Some growers cover the crown of lemon balm during the winter with a layer of ash or straw. This is a useful precaution, but from experience here at Harlow Car, on a cold uncompromising clay soil, merely leaving last season's foliage is sufficient.

LEMON VERBENA
Lippia citriodora *Verbenaceae*

Newcomers to gardening often confuse this plant with lemon balm, *Melissa officinalis*, although lemon balm is a fairly short-growing herbaceous plant, while lemon verbena is a woody shrub. Not reliably hardy in most of Britain, lemon verbena is generally grown as a conservatory plant. It is possible to grow it in the open, but it must inevitably be stooled, as lemon verbena is often cut back severely by the frost. For this reason, take it down to the ground each spring and allow basal shoots to develop and replace the wood that is removed. Old wood should be cut out irrespective of whether it is dead, in order to maintain a shapely and consistent plant. Unfortunately this does mean that the slender spikes of mauve

blossoms, usually produced during August, must be sacrificed. It is at this time that the foliage should be cut if you wish to dry it for later use in cakes and puddings, or as an ingredient of pot-pourri.

Being half-hardy, lemon verbena obviously benefits from being grown within the shelter of a wall or hedge. It also requires a free-draining soil that is not so rich that it promotes soft winter-vulnerable growth. Propagation is from soft-wood cuttings taken from non-flowering shoots during July and August. These root readily in a mixture of equal parts peat and sharp sand, the resulting plants being potted individually in John Innes Potting Compost No1 and overwintered in a greenhouse or on the window sill. Following hardening off, young plants can be planted out during May or early June.

LIQUORICE
Glycyrrhiza glabra *Leguminosae*

A well known product, but not a familiar garden plant, liquorice is a fascinating subject to grow. A shrubby-looking plant, but one of an herbaceous disposition, it has elegant pinnate foliage and racemes of mauve-coloured pea-like flowers from July until September. Although a perennial plant, liquorice root is not ready to harvest until three years old, so it is a doubtful proposition for all except the most patient. If you do fancy your chances of producing root liquorice, it is essential to have a deeply cultivated friable soil for the roots may penetrate down for 1m (3ft). That is not to say that it will not grow on heavier land, for it prospers on cold wet clay at Harlow Car. It is just that it is virtually impossible to remove the root intact from heavy land.

Commercially, liquorice is increased from small pieces of creeping stem which are dibbled into the soil during March. If you only require two or three plants, they are easily raised from seed sown during spring in a cold frame. Scatter slug pellets around the seedlings as they emerge, for liquorice seems to be a particular delicacy. As soon as the seedlings are large enough to handle, pot them individually in a good soil-less potting compost. If you can get hold of a few sweet-pea tubes in which to pot them, rather than conventional pots, then so much the better. These are usually made of the black, papery material, popularly referred to as whalehide, and are long, narrow and without a solid bottom. Being a member of the pea family, liquorice resents disturbance in much the same way that sweet peas do. Once the plants are well established, plant them in their permanent positions in full sun, ensuring that they are at least 45cm (18in) apart.

LOVAGE
Levisticum officinale *Umbelliferae*

Apart from its huge size, it is difficult to know why lovage has not become more popular amongst gardeners, for it is such a good herb. Its size need not be a handicap, for the plant can be kept within bounds by frequent cutting, especially of the towering 2 or 3m (6–9ft) high stems that support the rather uninspiring umbels of greenish-brown flowers. The handsome foliage is glaucous and divided into segments which are soft and aromatic when young. As they age, the leaves tend to become leathery and somewhat unpalatable, but never lose their strong celery aroma. Indeed, lovage can be used in almost every situation where one might consider celery for flavouring. Lovage tea is also said to be most invigorating.

Lovage is easily raised from seed, either sown in a pan on the window sill, or directly in the open ground if soil conditions permit. A March sowing is ideal for then the plants have an opportunity to attain a reasonable size before the end of the summer and thus permit the removal of a little foliage. If sown inside, it is important to move the seedlings into pots as soon as they are large enough to handle. Any good potting compost will suffice, but take care during potting not to damage the roots or disturb the seedlings unduly. Strong

young plants should be ready for planting out towards the end of June. If weather conditions are favourable, and direct sown lovage prospers, thin the seedlings to at least 60cm (2ft) apart, discarding the thinnings as they have little chance of transplanting and making satisfactory plants.

If you have an opportunity to propagate lovage from an existing plant, this can be done quite simply during early spring when strong young shoots are just appearing. These can be removed with a portion of root, potted in a good potting compost in small pots and allowed to establish within the protection of a cold frame. As the portions will have little root attached, it is important to water carefully until these have developed. Both dryness or over-watering can cause the demise of the divisions. Once the plants are well established in the pots, they can be planted out.

Lovage is an easy-going herb that prefers to grow in the open on a moisture-retentive soil. On heavy land it seems to grow particularly well, but if not carefully controlled will self-sow itself and become a nuisance. The ideal way of preventing this is to grow the plant merely for its foliage and cut out any flower stems as soon as they appear.

LUNGWORT
Pulmonaria officinalis *Boraginaceae*

This old herb gets its name from the time when it was believed that a herb looked like the disorder it was intended to cure, the leaves of pulmonarias being said to resemble lungs. Apart from its use in herb tea for the cure of chest complaints, this delightful garden plant has not in recent times been considered as a serious herbal subject. It is of the right physical disposition, however, to make a valuable contribution to the herb patch and is welcomed by most gardeners not only there, but in other shady parts of the garden where a tidy ground-cover plant is required.

There are many varieties of lungwort, some with blossoms in vivid hues. These I feel are out of keeping with a herb garden, so are omitted here. The important one for our purposes is the old-fashioned perennial soldiers and sailors, *Pulmonaria officinalis*. This has flowers which are rose-pink in bud, open mauve and then change to blue. It has rather coarse, bristly green leaves, splashed with greyish or silver patches. A tough perennial, it is easily increased by division during the winter, although you have a better chance of judging the liveliest portions of the plant if this is delayed until growth starts in the early spring. The time at which division of the plants can be undertaken is very limited, for pulmonarias spring from winter dormancy to full flower within a couple of weeks.

Lungwort
Pulmonaria officinalis

MARIGOLD, POT

Calendula officinalis Compositae

Even the rawest novice gardener is likely to be familiar with the pot marigold or calendula which is a common annual in gardens throughout the country, sporting vivid orange or yellow daisy-like flowers amongst strongly aromatic coarse green foliage.

Fewer are likely to realise that this was once an important herb and an important source of yellow dye. The blossoms were used in both medicine and cooking, being added to salads, broths and soups. So not only are they decorative, but useful too. The common species, and cultivars like Orange King not far removed, are the ones most suited to the herb garden. Modern brash cultivars are much too stiff and informal and now in colours that would be out of sympathy with the herb garden concept.

Calendula is easy to raise from seed sown where it is intended to flower. Although an annual, in most gardens it becomes a permanent feature perpetuating readily from self-sown seed. With this in mind, avoid modern hybrid cultivars, for progeny yielded from them are unlikely to bear any resemblance to their parents.

Providing that the soil is in reasonable condition, seed can be sown from early March onwards, the seedlings being thinned when convenient to 20cm apart in each direction. Apart from keeping calendulas weed free, little needs to be done until they flower and you are ready to garner a harvest. Mildew sometimes plagues the foliage of the older kinds – if so, spray at three-weekly intervals with a systemic fungicide based upon benomyl.

MARJORAM

Origanum majorana, O.onites, O.vulgare
Labiatae

If you are really ruthless about growing only the best in your garden, only one of the three marjorams is really worth considering. This is the perennial pot marjoram, *Origanum onites*. The other two have disadvantages which make them inferior as garden plants, and, as the foliage of these is not noticeably superior in any way, it makes sense, if you only have limited space, to choose the most compact and long-lived species.

Pot marjoram is grown from seed sown in a pan and given the protection of a frame during March. Use a good seed compost and prick the seedlings out when large enough to handle, moving them to pots before planting out during late May or early June. If you have an existing plant it is possible to root cuttings of the young vigorous shoots which appear in early spring. Short cuttings root quickly and freely in a pan containing a mixture of equal parts peat and sharp sand. Plant the young plants out, allowing about 30cm (1ft) between plants in each direction.

Apart from its usefulness as a herb, consider the pot marjoram also as a possible subject for the front of the flower border where its attractive clusters of deep mauve flowers can serve as a restaurant for every passing honey bee. Flower production obviously depresses foliage quality, but it is a small price to pay for the pleasure of watching the antics of bees at work amongst the blossoms on warm summer days. As with all marjorams, the foliage is used for garnishing, mixing in stuffing and to accompany fish dishes.

There is no reason to neglect the other marjorams if you do have sufficient room to grow them. Certainly wild marjoram, *O.vulgare*, should be grown when there is room, for this is the herb oregano, the Latin name for marjoram being *origanum* and this being the root of the common name oregano. It is a perennial and should be treated in exactly the same manner as pot marjoram, except that, being a straggly and untidy plant, it needs a little more room to spread out.

Sweet or knotted marjoram, *O.majorana*, has a much more pungent fragrance than the other two, but, sadly, must be treated as a half-hardy annual in this country, unless grown in a pot on the kitchen window sill. It has similar flowers, but smaller greyish-green leaves, and much prefers a free-draining sandy soil in full sun, whereas the other two are a little more amenable and tolerate quite heavy soil and partial shade without flinching.

Apart from those that are grown primarily for culinary purposes, there is a golden-leafed marjoram known to gardeners as *O.aureum* which behaves in exactly the same manner as *O.onites*, surviving the winter unscathed. For adding a splash of gold to the herb garden this is unsurpassable.

MARSH MALLOW

Althaea officinalis Malvaceae

Formerly a very important plant, not only for the marsh mallow that was derived from its dried, powdered roots, but also for its medicinal properties, this is now very much a decorative herb plant. The only use to which it has been put in recent times is as a vegetable, the roots being boiled and the fresh green tops being included in salads. Otherwise, it is a pleasant hollyhock-like plant for the back of the herb border where its hoary green foliage and spires of pinkish-purple blossoms can provide a sombre background for more colourful characters.

Marsh Mallow
Althaea officinalis

Melilot
Melilotus officinalis

A native of coastal areas, marsh mallow enjoys a light free-draining soil. It is propagated easily by seed, either sown where it is to flower, or else raised in a pan with a good seed compost and a little protection. Either way germination will be quite rapid, the seedlings being quite amenable to transplanting or shuffling around to ensure a solid stand of plants. Established plants can be lifted and divided during the autumn, but the best results are obtained from seed-raised plants that are replaced regularly every three or four years.

MELILOT

Melilotus officinalis Leguminosae

This lovely biennial herb was introduced to Britain as a fodder crop and is now locally naturalised. It grows up to 1m (3ft) high with smooth erect stems, handsome trifoliate leaves and long racemes of sweetly scented, yellow, pea-like flowers. Rarely used as a medicinal herb nowadays, it is a great bee-plant, the Latin name of the plant literally translated as the honey lotus.

Like most leguminous plants *Melilotus* resents disturbance, so seed should be sown directly where it is intended to flower during early spring. The seedlings need to be thinned out to at least 20cm (8in) apart, the thinnings being discarded as they have very little chance of re-establishment. An easy-going plant, the melilot adapts well to most soils and situations, except deep shade.

MINT

Mentha spp. Labiatae

There are many different strains of the popular culinary green mint, *Mentha spicata*. Quite recently a major commercial processor of kitchen mint assessed the properties of at least 180 different clones and varieties! In the garden it matters little which strain is used, providing that it is kept free from mint rust. This troublesome disease is quite common and very debilitating, damaging the stems and foliage if not treated promptly. A rich growing medium seems to assist in preventing an outbreak of the disease, together with the regular rotation of the mint patch. If the tell-tale signs of rapidly wilting stems and foliage covered with vivid orange pustules are seen, the plants must be defoliated and the leaves and stems burnt. Underground stems can be lifted and washed free of soil prior to moving to another part of the garden. Any new shoots should be free of the disease as the rust rarely manifests itself below ground. Ordinary household mint should be planted in a place where its spread can be contained, for, like horseradish, it is a good servant but a poor master and rapidly invades areas to which it has no title, if soil conditions are good.

If you want to start off a fresh mint patch, the simplest way to begin is to visit the local greengrocer and pick up a sprig of cuttings. If these are bright and green, they will root readily and as they are of commercial stock, they are likely to be of a good clean productive strain. Cut off the bottoms of the cuttings beneath water level in a bowl of water, to prevent an airlock occurring in the stem, and then stand them in a glass of water out of the full sun. As soon as roots appear, the cuttings should be transferred to a good soil-less potting compost in individual small pots. Once they have made a small rootball, they can be planted out.

Apart from green culinary mint there are dozens of other kinds that crave attention, such as the richly scented ones like orange, ginger, pineapple and the ever popular Eau-de-Cologne type. The latter is a form of *M.citrata*, a handsome plant with branching stems and roughly oval, somewhat oily, dull green leaves, edged with purple, which fill the air with a sweet heady fragrance on a warm summer day. Then there is peppermint, *M.piperita*, one of the few mints that can be easily and successfully raised from seed. The form known as black peppermint is the finest of all, with dark green foliage on purple-bronze stems. If you want to use the leaves, avoid the white peppermint, *M.piperita officinalis*, for although it has attractive downy green leaves, it is much less hardy. Indeed, both peppermints need a little protection during the winter, for they tend to creep over the soil, rather than through it. A light covering of coarse moss peat is sufficient to ensure their survival.

Peppermint is grown for its leaves which are used in drinks, a fine oil also being extracted from the less palatable white peppermint.

Applemint, *M.rotundifolia*, appears at first glance to be of little culinary value either, for its pale, rounded, green leaves are soft and downy. It is, however, often used as a substitute for *M.spicata* and as a constituent of the drink mint-ale. A rather tall and lanky plant, it is seen at its most attractive in the more compact cream and green variegated *M.rotundifolia var.variegata*. This, along with the gold-and-green-leafed ginger mint, *M.gentilis*, adds a bit of colour and character to the herb border. There is no reason why mints should not be attractive as well as functional and an excursion through any good nursery catalogue will yield all kinds of interesting possibilities, including one of my favourites, the curly mint, *M.spicata crispata*.

If you have a wet patch in the herb garden, investigate the possibilities offered by the native water mint, *M.aquatica*. Of little culinary or medicinal value, this aromatic fellow has rampant, hairy, grey-green foliage and small dense whorls of pinkish-purple flowers. Invasive if not kept in check, it is one of the easiest mints to grow and seems remarkably tolerant of mint rust. So does pennyroyal, *M.pulegium*, a herb that nowadays is grown purely for decoration. With small, strongly aromatic foliage, it was once used by sailors to sweeten stale drinking water during long periods at sea.

All the mints are easily rooted from short stem cuttings taken at any time during the summer, and while some are occasionally offered as seed, the resulting plants are likely to be variable and not always particularly attractive. If you do grow mints from seed, then the seedlings require culling heavily.

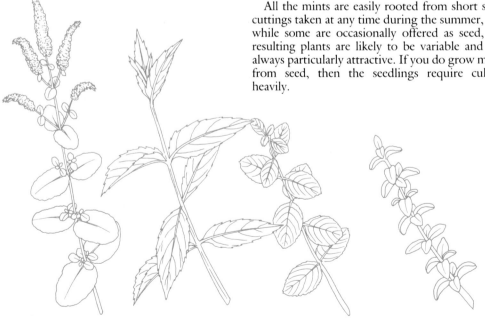

Applemint	Green culinary mint	Eau-de-Cologne mint	Pennyroyal
M. rotundifolia	*M. spicata*	*M. citrata*	*M. pulegium*

MOUNTAIN TOBACCO
Arnica montana *Compositae*
This is not a widely grown herb, but one occasionally encountered in the seedsman's catalogue. It
can be fairly readily raised from seed sown during
spring in pans of good seed compost, the seedlings
being transferred to small pots in John Innes
Potting Compost No1, for planting out during
mid-summer. A rather coarse, hardy perennial,
mountain tobacco can also be carefully divided
during the dormant winter period.

Preferring a position in the full sun or dappled
shade, this interesting, orange-flowered, daisy-like
plant is at home in any free-draining soil. Grown
now merely as a decorative plant, its flowers and
roots have, in the past, been gathered and dried
and are the main constituent of tincture of arnica, a
herbal cure for chilblains and cold sores.

MUGWORT
Artemisia vulgaris *Compositae*
This interesting native herb is of no great beauty,
but, when cultivated, provides a useful foil for
more colourful plants in the herb garden. A
somewhat shrubby perennial, closely allied to the
popular wormwood of gardeners, *Artemisia
absinthium*, it resembles this in most respects
except that its pinnately divided leaves are only
silvery beneath. A dull greyish-green above, these
are borne on coarse reddish or purple stems which
give rise to slender spires of insignificant purplish
flowers.

Growing on any soil in most situations except
dense shade, mugwort is a very versatile plant
which is easily propagated by winter division, or
short stem cuttings taken as they emerge through
the soil during early spring. These cuttings root
readily in an equal parts mixture of peat and sharp
sand, the young plants being established in small
pots of any good potting compost before planting
out in their permanent positions.

Although no longer used by the modern cook or
herbalist, mugwort has had an important past,
especially as a substitute for tea. It was also used in
the flavouring of beer, for seasoning poultry and as
a cure for epilepsy and tapeworm, as well as in the
making of medicinal pillows.

MYRTLE
Myrtus communis *Myrtaceae*
This is one of the loveliest shrubby plants, yielding
a rich fragrance. It is a handsome evergreen which,
in favoured parts of the country, can grow into
quite a sizeable tree. It is not reliably hardy in the
north of England and here, at Harlow Car
Gardens, it has to be treated as a plant for the
unheated greenhouse. Where it can successfully be
grown in the open, it is tolerant of any free-
draining soil in a sunny position.

Myrtle can be readily increased from short
cuttings of lateral shoots, taken with a heel during
September and rooted within the protection of a
cold frame or the kitchen window sill. Use a
mixture of equal parts by volume of peat and sharp
sand or peat and perlite and be sure to dip the ends
of the cuttings in a hormone rooting powder. It
will generally be March or April before the
cuttings have rooted sufficiently to be potted up.
At this stage it is important to use a soil-based
compost such as John Innes No1. Soil-less composts, unless watering is very carefully controlled,
cause leaf-drop of freshly rooted cuttings.

It is wise to grow the plants on for a season in
pots before planting out. Grow them on hard in
the John Innes No1 which, while it does not
promote lusty growth, does yield tough plants

Myrtle
Myrtus communis

whose constitution more readily ensures survival. For much of the country myrtle cannot be considered as a reliable proposition outdoors, except during the summer months. Pot culture presents no difficulties providing that the plants are grown in John Innes Potting Compost No3 and kept outside for the summer months. Although resenting the damp and cold of the British winter, myrtle is equally intolerant of hot tropical conditions.

As a herb, myrtle yields little of merit. However, it has a long tradition bound up with weddings and the mystique with which country people surrounded them. Myrtle is dedicated to Venus and in the language of flowers its message is love. As a matter of course, every bride had to have a sprig of myrtle in her wedding bouquet and it was from these sprigs that myrtle bushes were established in many old cottage gardens, the tradition being that they should be planted by the bridesmaid.

In practical terms it is an invaluable foliage subject, providing excellent long-lasting cut material for the flower arranger.

NASTURTIUM
Tropaeolum majus, T.minus *Tropaeolaceae*
The common garden nasturtiums are popular and colourful herb plants, the leaves, petals and seeds being used freely in salads where they impart a hot peppery flavour. Nasturtiums are also very useful in the garden, especially on impoverished soils in full sun. Here they will scramble around, flaunting brilliant red, orange and yellow blossoms of tropical exuberance. If you want to enjoy their flowers as well as use their foliage be sure that you give them a poor soil. High fertility results in luxuriant foliage, rampant growth and few flowers.

Of annual duration, nasturtiums are easily and quickly raised from seed sown directly into open ground. The soil should be well prepared and friable, the large pea-like seeds being planted at their final spacings, 10cm (4in) apart. Nasturtiums germinate freely and without difficulty, so it is rare that gaps are caused by failures. Even when an odd seed does fail to emerge, its neighbours soon close the area of bare soil with their creeping foliage. Although easily grown, nasturtiums are frost tender and it is therefore unwise to sow the seeds before the end of April.

Cultivation demands little effort, as nasturtiums look after themselves, but an eye should be kept open for blackfly as this often plagues the succulent foliage. When spotted, apply a good systemic insecticide immediately, noting the period that must elapse between spraying and harvesting if you are going to eat the foliage. If merely for decoration this is of little account. Apart from that there are no cultural worries, although it is useful if, when frost blackens the foliage, you rake it up immediately, together with the rounded green fruits. While the foliage of nasturtiums is frost-tender, the seeds seem remarkably hardy and are quite capable of overwintering in the soil. This can be a nuisance if you are not planning on having nasturtiums in the same place the following year.

There are many cultivars of garden nasturtium, all of which can be utilised in the herb garden. However, many of the modern kinds are so brash that they do not fit easily into the concept of a herb garden held by most gardeners. So tend to choose ordinary, mixed kinds without fancy names, selecting either the scrambling or compact sorts, according to situation. It is the scrambling or climbing nasturtium which is traditionally grown, but if you are restricted in space, compact strains like 'Tom Thumb' are quite acceptable.

ONION GREEN
Allium fistulosum *Liliaceae*
A relative of chives and used in a similar way, onion green, or Welsh onions, are an invaluable addition to the herb garden. Of a stronger flavour than chives, the chopped leaves of this hardy perennial need to be used with great care in seasoning dishes. While not as attractive as chives in appearance, having thicker foliage and paltry whitish flowers, onion green is nevertheless tougher and in most gardens can provide foliage for much of the year.

Onion green is easy to grow on any reasonable soil, providing that it is not heavily shaded. Like chives it is easily increased by division and, while it can be grown informally in the herb garden, it is more often accommodated on the vegetable patch, the plants being grown 30cm (1ft) apart with 45cm (18in) between rows. Apart from keeping free of weeds, onion green demands little attention except the removal of flower heads as soon as they appear. This helps to maintain the quality of the foliage.

ORACHE
Atriplex hortensis *Chenopodiaceae*
This is a herb often offered by seedsmen, but it is not amongst the herbs that you will find it listed, for it is more commonly grown as a colourful foliage annual plant. Its use as a herb has largely diminished, following the improvement of spinach as a leafy vegetable. Indeed, nowadays it is rarely encountered in its ordinary green-leafed form, but more often appears in cream and crimson foliage varieties which are not quite so hardy.

Ordinary orache is a herb akin to Good King

Henry, but growing 1m (3ft) or more high on favourable soils and, unlike that plant, of annual duration. Its cultural requirements are similar and its foliage likewise utilised as a substitute for spinach. Once cultivated in rows on the vegetable plot, it is now more frequently encountered towards the rear of the herb border where it provides a pleasant foil for more colourful herbs. The selected coloured-leafed forms can be used to good effect in the herb border if you are not a purist, but they are not truly plants of the herbal tradition and are not quite as resilient either, being best raised in seed trays before planting out.

The seed should ideally be sown during early March in a cold frame, using a good seed compost and the seedlings being pricked out as soon as they are large enough to handle. Once established, they can be planted out in their summer quarters. This should be around the middle of May, the young plants being spaced 15–20cm (6–8in) apart and then kept well watered until properly at home. If you are going to grow the ordinary green-leafed kind, then seed can be sown directly in the place where it is to grow during early April, thinning the seedlings once they have reached a reasonable size to handle.

Orache is a very amenable plant, tolerating most situations except dense shade. Soil conditions are not critical either, for on hostile dry soils it will mature at about 60cm (2ft), without looking haggard, yet in a rich organic medium will grow over 1m (3ft) with large arrow-like foliage of great luxuriance.

ORRIS

Iris florentina *Iridaceae*
This is the lovely, early white-flowered iris of the traditional cottage garden. It is a beautifully scented plant which associates so well with the fiery orange of Siberian wallflowers in the late spring garden. However, it is as a herbal and symbolic plant that it has been important. A sign of faith, wisdom and valour, the orris root was formerly an economic plant of great significance in herbal medicine, perfumery and snuff-making.

In our gardens today it is an attractive and much-loved garden flower, associating well with other herb plants, its bold sword-shaped leaves providing a valuable architectural quality, while its pristine blossoms fill the air with sweet fragrance. Growing easily on any free-draining soil, it must have a position in full sun. Treat it as you would ordinary bearded or German irises and success is assured.

Plant directly after flowering, lifting congested clumps of rhizomes and selecting vigorous young individuals from the outer portion of the plant.

Even if smaller than rhizomes from the centre portion, they ultimately make much better individuals. Trim back the adult leaves to about a third of their length and reduce any trailing roots. The rhizomes can then be planted in a well-drained soil, preferably of an alkaline tendency. Ensure that wherever possible they are planted in a north to south direction. This ensures that the bold fans of leaves do not shade the rhizomes which, to prosper, require all the sun that they can get. At planting time watch out for any signs of rhizome-rot. This is a troublesome disease not uncommon amongst plants that are congested or growing on badly-drained soil. Always remove and burn any diseased rhizomes. These are easily recognised by soft, somewhat gelatinous and evil-smelling patches which invade the tissue and ultimately cause collapse of the foliage.

Orris
Iris florentina

PARSLEY

Petroselinum crispum *Umbelliferae*

This is undoubtedly the best known of the culinary herbs and subject to many superstitions. In years gone by it was very much a medicinal herb rather than one for culinary use. Parsley tea was used up until the First World War for kidney troubles, an ointment of parsley leaves and snails was utilised by the French for treating swellings, and the well-known oil, apiol, was extracted from the seeds. In addition it had symbolic meaning to the ancient Greeks who crowned victors at the Isthmian Games with chaplets of parsley and also made wreaths of it for their tombs.

With such a history you would think that there would be no mystery about its cultivation. However, this is not so, for even today gardeners regale one another with tales about its unpredictability. It is said that parsley goes down to visit the devil seven times before appearing above ground and that to transplant parsley is bad luck.

Although the stories attached to parsley are quite obviously traditional, they have arisen in some cases from the plant's behaviour. Parsley seed is of very short viability and unless fresh seeds are sown, there is little chance of a high percentage germination. In most cases seed that is a year old has no chance at all of being viable, unless packaged in modern airtight, foil packets. Even fresh seed gives gardeners a headache, because it takes several weeks to germinate and, if sown in a cold damp soil in the spring, is likely to rot rather than germinate.

All these complications have led to a rash of theories concerning the germination of parsley seed. The commonest and most damaging is that parsley seeds should have boiling water poured over them to hasten germination. This does no good at all and in most cases kills the seed completely. An alternative theory is to pour boiling water along the opened drills before parsley seed is sown. This does no harm, in fact it helps to sterilise the soil, but it will have little, if any, bearing upon the germination of the seed. Old seed and cold damp soil are the most frequent causes of failure. If these can be overcome, parsley is no more difficult than any other popular culinary herb.

The usual recommendation for parsley is to sow it where it is to grow during March or April, making shallow drills, or, in the informal herb border, broadcasting the seeds and raking them in. On light, free-draining soil this works well providing that you use fresh seed. The seedlings emerge in four to six weeks and, as soon as the first rough leaves are showing, can be thinned to 15cm (6in) apart in each direction. This will soon give complete cover of the soil with foliage. In a more formal situation, such as in the vegetable plot where more than a single row is growing, it is useful to give at least 30cm (1ft) between rows to allow for regular cultivation.

On heavier soils it is possible to follow the same routine as outlined for gardeners on well-drained soils, but the results will be very hit and miss. If the soil happens to be caught at just the right time and succeeding weather is kind, it is certainly possible to raise a good stand. The odds against this, however, are great, so I favour the raising of young plants in a good seed compost in a frame or on the window sill, potting them up, and then planting them out when both weather and soil conditions are more favourable. This needs doing with great care, for parsley resents disturbance and is given to running straight into flower if not carefully handled. As soon as the first rough, rounded leaf appears between the two lance-like seed leaves, carefully lift each seedling with as much compost as possible and transfer them to small peat pots. If you sow the seeds into a fairly coarse soil-less compost, it is often easier to lift a reasonable rootball. Water the transplanted seedlings well and place them in a cold frame, ensuring that they do not dry out at any time. They can be planted in their permanent positions as soon as their roots have filled the pots.

Although parsley can be tricky to grow from seed on heavy land, once established it prospers. Indeed, it seems to grow better on a moisture-retentive soil rather than a free-draining kind, the foliage often turning a creamy or pinkish colour in dry conditions. This is an indicator of stress, but can be caused by other factors, including carrot fly. If such an attack is noticed, the plants are best discarded. In my experience it so rarely happens that, apart from adding a standard seed dressing to the seeds before sowing in open ground, few other precautions need be taken. Dryness is a greater problem and attention to watering must be constantly given to plants on light soils or in containers. Failure to attend to this will result in the plants running to seed prematurely. In any event parsley is a biennial and therefore the best foliage is always produced the first year. Immediately its metabolism turns to flower production, foliage quality rapidly deteriorates. This is why many gardeners treat parsley as an annual and replace it each year. The main benefit of growing it on into the second season is that it can be covered with a cloche in January or February and fresh foliage cut in March and April. As long as any emerging flower spikes are removed as soon as noticed, the quality of foliage will be quite acceptable.

There are many different cultivars of parsley, but only two different types. The plain-leafed or French parsley is generally accepted as being as close to the species as we will come, while the moss-curled kinds are generally referred to in botanical circles as *var. foliosum*, although some authorities place the so-called true French parsley with caraway and call it *Carum petroselinum*. The botanical complexities need not concern us here, for all that are in cultivation today are unquestionably selections and hybrids. All the gardener needs to worry about is the difference between plain and curled parsley. The former is of a coarser, more vulgar appearance, usually with very dark green, shiny, divided foliage, whereas the leaves of the moss-curled kinds are crimpled and ruffled around the edge, often deeply divided and a much paler or brighter green, rarely with a glossy surface. Both are used for garnishing and seasoning, the plain-leafed kind having the reputation of being more pungent. While there are unquestionably selections of the plain-leafed kind in cultivation, none have apparently been given cultivar names, so when you buy seeds they will just be called French plain-leafed parsley. The moss-curled kinds, on the other hand, come with a plethora of names. Many of the modern kinds are even and compact, but otherwise the foliage is very much the same. Any cultivar offered by a leading seedhouse is likely to be perfectly satisfactory.

As intimated earlier, fresh parsley foliage can be gathered throughout the summer and early autumn following a spring sowing. It can also be obtained fresh during early spring if given the protection of a cloche. At other times only dried or frozen foliage is available, unless you are able to keep several pots growing on the window sill. If you wish to dry parsley foliage, gather only good quality leaves during the height of the summer growing season. If dried quickly, this is not only a superior quality to that gathered at other times, but also retains its fresh green colour much better.

PARSLEY, HAMBURG
Petroselinum sativum Umbelliferae

This is perhaps more correctly a vegetable than a herb, although its strongly aromatic foliage can be used as a parsley substitute, especially in soups and stews. With leaves like parsley and a root like a parsnip, yet no larger than a carrot, this is the ideal multi-purpose herb or vegetable for the small garden. It is the roots for which it is cultivated, having the texture of young carrots but the flavour of parsnip, and making excellent eating either fried or mixed in a vegetable stew.

Hamburg parsley must be sown in the open ground where it is to mature. By its very nature it

Parsley
Petroselinum crispum

is better accommodated in the vegetable garden than the herb border, for it is easier managed when grown in neat rows. Sow the seed during March and April in shallow drills 30cm (1ft) apart where the plants are to mature. As the seedlings emerge and produce their first rough leaves, thin them to 10cm (4in) apart. The plants should grow on happily if kept well watered and weed-free, the roots being lifted during the autumn and winter as required, although it is useful to have a few roots stored in a box of peat in a cool frost-free place for when winter weather makes the outdoor crop impossible to lift. In any event, it is wise to lift the remains of the crop before the end of the year in case a day or two of mild weather encourages re-growth. This quickly spoils the roots which become woody and unpalatable.

PURSLANE
Portulaca oleracea *Portulacaceae*

Purslane is an easily grown annual herb most commonly used, in its young stage, fresh in salads, although older foliage is sometimes included in stews. Together with sorrel, it is a constituent of the French soup called *bonne femme*. In days gone by it was used as a medicinal herb, reputedly curing 'heat in the liver' and 'pains in the head'. Legend also has it that purslane is a protection against evil spirits and 'blastings by lightning'. The common kind is an untidy, but happy plant, with smooth rounded leaves and somewhat procumbent stems. Along with the closely related, but less robust, golden purslane, *P.sativa*, it makes a cheerful and useful addition to the herb garden.

Purslane is easily grown from seed sown directly where it is to grow, thinning the seedlings to 15cm (6in) apart once the first rough leaves are showing. Do not sow too early, late April or early May being soon enough on all but the lightest of soils. However, purslane is not the ideal subject for light free-draining soils as it is quickly stressed through lack of moisture. If you have a dry soil, water the plants freely or else they will quickly deteriorate. Young shoots can be picked for salads as soon as large enough, sufficient growth being allowed to remain on each plant to provide more mature foliage later in the season.

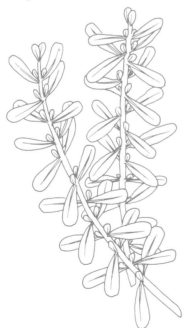

Purslane
Portulaca oleracea

ROSEMARY
Rosmarinus officinalis *Labiatae*

Along with parsley, mint and thyme this is probably the best-known and widest cultivated of herbs. Not just for its strongly aromatic foliage which is used in meat dishes, but as a decorative garden plant, for it has attractive greyish-green foliage with white undersides and spires of beautiful blue blossoms during May and early June. The ordinary species grows upwards of 1m (3ft) high, even taller in mild south western coastal districts, eventually forming an unruly conical mound. The cultivar popularly called 'Miss Jessop's Variety' and now more correctly referred to as 'Fastigiatus' is the neatest grower, having a strong, upright, pyramidal habit rather like a small conifer. This also has blue flowers and is the same as the variety offered under the name 'Pyramidalis'. 'Benenden Blue' is a smaller-growing cultivar with very narrow dark green leaves and bright blue flowers, while 'Roseus' has pink blossoms, and 'Albus' white. For the gardener with limited space 'Severn Sea' is a joy, with slender arching branches smothered in brilliant blue blossoms. This is the best rosemary for pot cultivation, being both a decorative and culinary plant. For protected cultivation there is also the lovely scrambling *R.lavandulaceus*. In Yorkshire it is not hardy, but has grown happily for a number of years in a large pot in an unheated greenhouse.

All varieties of rosemary enjoy a sunny well-drained position, and although in cooler northern areas, on heavy soils, they often suffer die-back during the winter, they usually regenerate quickly from old wood. Flowering suffers, however, for it is only on growth made during the previous season that flowers are produced. Bear this in mind when pruning, although not much formal pruning is necessary, merely the shaping and tidying up of the bush in spring. Rosemary enjoys fairly harsh soil conditions, so use no more than an annual application of bonemeal in the spring to sustain growth. Heavy fertiliser applications lead to die-back and blackening of the foliage, a not infrequent sight in garden centres where young plants are container-grown in a standard soil-less potting medium. Young rosemary plants should only be grown in a soil-based compost, so choose one with a low nutrient content like John Innes Potting Compost No1.

Rosemary can be grown from seed or cuttings, the latter method being the only way in which named varieties can be perpetuated. Seed is only for the common species, *Rosmarinus officinalis*, and even then is an unreliable method, for although the seeds germinate freely, the seedlings damp off regularly, especially when grown in a soil-less compost. The only chance of success is to sow seeds in John Innes Seed Compost during March and April in a cold frame. Too warm conditions, especially associated with high humidity, such as is found on the kitchen window sill, will encourage the delicate seedlings to rot off. Prick out emerging seedlings, as soon as they are large enough to handle, in John Innes Potting Compost No1, moving them on again when large enough to be transferred to small pots. During this period it is important to keep them cool and water sparingly.

The same growing-on technique applies for plants raised from cuttings. Selected, short, lateral growths of the current season are removed with a heel of old wood during July or early August. Use a hormone rooting preparation and insert the cuttings in an equal parts by volume mixture of peat and sharp sand and once again utilise a cold frame. The same growing conditions suggested for seeds apply to cuttings. The failure rate will be higher than one might expect for such a popular plant, as at least half are likely to succumb under the conditions usually available to the home gardener. So take twice as many cuttings as you think that you will need at the outset. Young plants from either seed or cuttings are best over-wintered in a frame for planting out the following spring. If you have difficulty with either seeds or cuttings, it is sometimes possible to layer a low-growing branch from a mature plant.

Rue
Ruta graveolens

Rosemary
Rosmarinus officinalis

RUE
Ruta graveolens Rutaceae

Although a most attractive addition to the herb garden, rue is not nowadays used popularly as a herb. It has no culinary value, its attributes being associated with its alleged ability to cure eye ailments, flatulence, disorders in women and various diseases in cattle. To most people it has an unpleasant odour, but some find it agreeable. It is certainly not a fragrant herb, its pungent aroma reminding me of over-ripe Gorgonzola cheese. Notwithstanding the desirability or otherwise of its smell, it is a welcome addition to the herb garden, being an easy-going perennial with handsome, deeply cut, blue-green foliage that is evergreen in most seasons. In severe winters older plants sometimes lose their leaves, but, surprisingly, young ones rarely do. A small shrubby plant best suited to a free-draining soil in a sheltered position, it will ultimately attain a height of 45–60cm (18–24in) and, during the summer months, produce clusters of nondescript yellowish or greenish flowers. Its foliage is its main attribute, especially that of the lovely steely-blue cultivar 'Jackman's Blue'. This needs to be vegetatively propagated, unlike the strange cream and blue-green variegated 'Variegata' which, surprisingly for a variegated subject, comes absolutely true from seed.

Indeed, seed is the easiest way of raising the ordinary rue also. It germinates freely if sown during March or April in a good seed compost and provided with a little protection. A cold frame or unheated greenhouse would be ideal, but the kitchen window sill will do. It is best pricked out as soon as the first rough leaf has developed and, once established in the seed tray, should be potted on into small pots. Rue that becomes root-bound in a tray rarely makes it when planted out. Growth is fairly rapid and sizeable plants can be obtained for planting out during late June or July from a March or April sowing. Rue can also be increased from cuttings of young shoots taken during June and July. Indeed, it is the only method of reproducing a selected foliage cultivar like 'Jackman's Blue'. Use a mixture of equal parts by volume of peat and sharp sand or peat and perlite, and provide the protection of a cold frame or window sill. Rooting will take at least three or four weeks, following which the cuttings should be potted individually, preferably in John Innes Potting Compost No1, and given the protection of a cold frame for the winter months. They can be planted out in the spring as soon as soil conditions are suitable.

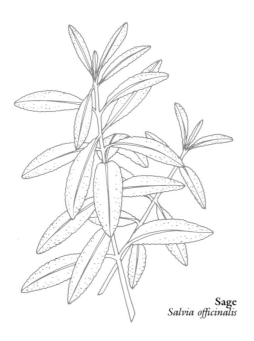

Sage
Salvia officinalis

SAGE
Salvia officinalis Labiatae

An all-time favourite amongst culinary herbs, sage is found in gardens throughout the country, cultivated for its attractive grey-green, rough-textured foliage which is such an important ingredient in stuffings and meat dishes. Formerly it was regarded as an important medicinal plant, being used as an astringent and a stimulant, although its use in this field is now largely confined to making soothing sage tea. In the herb garden it serves a decorative purpose too, especially the coloured-leafed forms which are favoured by some herbalists. If you are growing sage primarily for culinary use, then it is the selected, so-called broad-leaved sage that you use which is merely an improved form of the common *Salvia officinalis*. In addition to this there is a white-flowered form called *S.o.var.albiflora* which yields delicate spires of pure white blossoms, an unexpected contrast when planted alongside the ordinary blue-flowered sort. Not that either should be allowed to flower if you expect to get the finest quality foliage. Amongst the coloured foliage kinds there is the red sage, *S.o.* 'Purpurescens', with handsome purplish leaves, golden sage, *S.o.*'Icterina' with lovely striated golden foliage, and the somewhat bizarre purple, grey-green, pink and white *S.o.*'Tricolor' which sports leaves like a painter's palette.

Common sage can be readily grown from seed sown during March and April in a good seed compost. Either kind gives good results, but I find that with John Innes Seed Compost the watering is easier to control, an important factor when raising sage from seed, as young plants are very vulnerable to damping-off. Indeed, it is a wise precaution to use Cheshunt Compound in the water as a standard precaution. A weekly dose should do much to keep this disease at bay. Prick the seedlings out as soon as they are large enough to handle and grow them on in John Innes Potting Compost No 1. When they are able to cope with life in small pots, pot them up using the same medium. A spring sowing should produce plants that can be planted out in June or July. Of course, if you have an established sage bush, then you can increase from cuttings. It is a good policy to do so every few years in any event as sage will become woody and unruly despite careful and regular pruning. Take the current season's growth, removing short shoots with a heel of the old wood during June and July. Use a rooting hormone and dip the cut surface of each cutting in this. Insert in a mixture of equal parts peat and sharp sand, or peat and perlite, and place the cuttings in a frame or on the window sill. Ensure that the rooting medium remains moist, but do not get water on the foliage as this causes the leaves to blacken and drop off. Rooting takes place in three to four weeks. Thereafter get the plants potted and treat them in the same way as transplanted seedlings. Cuttings are the only reliable way of increasing the coloured-leafed kinds.

Sage is a Mediterranean plant and therefore benefits from an open sunny position on a well-drained soil. It is perfectly hardy and, although it occasionally loses its foliage during the winter, this can more often than not be attributed to dampness rather than cold. For culinary use the leaves of sage can be cut at any time during the summer growing season, providing that you remove the flowers. If you wish to enjoy the spikes of attractive blue blossoms, then cease cutting just before they bloom during midsummer. Early shoots are the best when selecting sage for drying.

SALAD BURNET
Sanguisorba minor *Rosaceae*
This is an interesting, rather than decorative, hardy perennial herb plant with strange greenish, eventually reddish, knobbly flowers on wiry stems about 30cm (1ft) high. These sit on top of mounds of grey-green compound leaves which impart a cucumber-like tang. It is for this quality that the leaves are gathered, making an invaluable addition to the salad dish. The fresh foliage of young plants is always of better quality than that produced by older woody plants, so it is advisable to replace your plants every three or four years. If you wish to obtain the best from cut foliage, prevent the strange, rounded flower heads from being produced, nipping out the emerging buds as soon as noticed. The leaves of salad burnet do not dry well, but this is of little account, for it is almost evergreen and there are always pickings to be had during the winter months, although these are likely to be coarser and impart a sharper, bitter flavour.

Salad burnet is one of the easiest herbs to grow, tolerating all manner of soils and seeding freely if allowed to do so. Although it can be easily grown from a direct sowing in the open ground, I prefer to raise the plants in pots and then plant them in their permanent positions. This ensures a good uniform batch of plants and the minimal extra time expended is well rewarded. Sow the seed in a good seed compost during March or April, in a frame or on the window sill. The resulting plants will be ready to put out towards the end of June or early July. It is possible to divide the coarse woody rootstock in the autumn, but I do not favour this, as the resulting plants are variable in growth and the leaves do not have the succulence of those produced by young seed-raised plants.

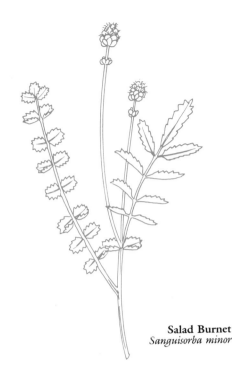

Salad Burnet
Sanguisorba minor

SAVORY, SUMMER
Satureja hortensis *Labiatae*
This is a pretty annual herb with slender erect stems 30cm (1ft) or so high, narrow green leaves and pale pink axillary blossoms during July. It is a most attractive bee-plant if allowed to develop properly, but, if used in the kitchen, the leading succulent shoots should be removed during June, just prior to flowering. It is used extensively in meat dishes and for flavouring soups and stews. In years gone by summer savory was used as a cure for insect stings, the shoots being bruised and the juice spread over the inflamed area.

It is not a particularly easy herb to grow, for it germinates irregularly and young plants can collapse without warning in damp ground. Recommendations to sow summer savory directly outside in a seed bed during April are fraught with difficulties unless you are gardening on a light, well-drained soil. If you are, then sow thinly and rationalise the resulting seedlings to 10cm (4in) apart. For the majority who garden on medium and heavy soils, I suggest raising the plants with a little protection and using John Innes Seed Compost rather than any of the soil-less kinds.

Plants grown in soil-less compost always show a tendency to damp off, despite regular applications of Cheshunt Compound. In fact I am not sure whether it is the damping-off disease that causes

Summer Savory
Satureja hortensis

Winter Savory
Satureja montana

the problem, or merely that summer savory dislikes peat-based composts. However, once the seedlings have germinated, prick them out two or three to a small pot, eventually thinning to the strongest plant. Do not prick out into trays and then move the plants into pots as they dislike disturbance, although I have found that you can get away with it in the early seedling stage. Respectable plants can be planted out towards the end of May.

SAVORY, WINTER
Satureja montana Labiatae
Unlike its summer counterpart, winter savory is a hardy, somewhat shrubby perennial which, at first glance, looks rather like a well-grown thyme. It has always been a culinary plant, being used in every kind of cooking where a warm spicy flavour was desired. It can be used fresh at any time during the summer, but young shoots taken during May are the most flavoursome. These are the ones that should be harvested for drying, although culinary experts declare that dried winter savory leaves are hard and unpalatable. The best thing to do, therefore, is to give a plant or two the protection of a cloche so that fresh foliage can be harvested all the year through.

Winter savory is an easy-going plant that benefits from an open sunny situation, but tolerates most soils. One of the most frequent recommendations is to grow it on poor, hungry soil. While I cannot endorse such action, it is true that winter savory does best without heavy fertil-

ising and prospers on lighter well-drained land. Seed-raising is simple, the seed being sown in its final position during April and the emerging seedlings being thinned out to 20cm (8in) apart. The first useful cuttings of foliage for the kitchen are not normally made until the following season.

Cuttings can be used as a means of propagation, young side shoots with a heel of old wood being taken during June and rooted in a mixture of equal parts peat and sharp sand, or peat and perlite. They root within two or three weeks and should be potted up using John Innes Potting Compost No2 and accommodated in a frame until the spring, although, on light soils, it is often possible to establish young plants successfully in the open ground during September and October. Apart from its culinary value, winter savory responds well to clipping and can be used to make tiny hedges in small formal herb gardens. In addition to the common kind there is a creeping savory called *S.montana var.subspicata* and an upright form known as *S.m.var.communis*.

SELF-HEAL
Prunella vulgaris Labiatae
A cheery native plant, this is no longer used as a herb, but can still be usefully accommodated in the herb garden. It is a rambling perennial, no more than 15cm (6in) high with blunt, hairy, green leaves and bluish-purple lipped flowers. It is easily grown under harsh conditions and increases readily from division during the winter months.

SOAPWORT

Saponaria officinalis Caryophyllaceae

Most gardeners who grow this do so for its untidy heaps of dull green foliage and pink or deep rose blossoms. It is truly a cottage-garden plant, being known by country folk as Bouncing Bet and having been maintained in cultivation since Roman times. Originally it was grown for its economic value rather than any decorative merits, the foliage being used to make a particularly fine kind of soap. Even today, those involved in the cleaning and restoring of old tapestries and textiles use an extract from this plant in their work.

As a garden plant it has great merit, making a useful and colourful addition to the late spring and early summer herb border. While it can be lifted, divided and spread about during the autumn and winter months, it is just as easy to raise from seed, the resulting plants being of much better habit. Either sow in the position in which it is to remain during March and April, or in a good seed compost in a frame or on the window ledge. Pot the young plants up when large enough to be accommodated in small pots. These will be big enough to plant out during June from a March sowing. Soapwort likes an open sunny position in almost any soil that does not become waterlogged during winter.

SORREL

Rumex scutatus Polygonaceae

The sorrel grown for culinary use is the so-called French sorrel, although some early gardening books and herbals recommend the culture of our native sorrel *R.acetosa*. Constant reselection of the former has resulted in a strain popularly known as 'French Broad-leafed'. Of similar appearance to our native dock, *R.obtusifolius*, this has broader smoother leaves of vivid green. Well-grown French sorrel leaves are tender, of a rather acidic flavour, and can be used in salads and soups, or cooked like spinach.

A perennial, it is easily increased by division during early spring. When a larger number of plants are required, they can be raised from seeds sown in the open ground during March or April. Being vigorous growers they require planting at least 30cm (1ft) apart. Few problems beset the grower of sorrel, for it tolerates a wide range of soil types and is only troubled by slugs. These frequently attack succulent young shoots during early spring, but can be readily controlled by using modern showerproof slug pellets scattered amongst the plants. A circle of weathered soot around each plant is also a useful slug deterrent.

If a regular supply of leaves is required throughout the summer, it is important to remove the flower spikes immediately they are seen. In any event, it is prudent to remove them before the seed ripens and they get scattered about, for unwanted seedlings can become a nuisance. Sorrel cannot be successfully dried and stored; it must always be used fresh.

Soapwort
Saponaria officinalis

Sorrel
Rumex scutatus

SOUTHERNWOOD
Artemisia abrotanum *Compositae*

Another popular name for this old favourite is lad's love, alluding to the belief that this herb has the power to promote the growth of hair on the faces of adolescent youths. Ageing males also attempted to restore receding hairlines with the same herb. It has been used medicinally as a wound herb, a cure for worms and quite genuinely as a dye plant for wool, imparting a rich yellow colour. Never having been used for culinary purposes, it is essentially a decorative plant.

A somewhat shrubby character, southernwood is best treated as an herbaceous perennial and cut to ground level every year. At Harlow Car we do this in the spring, so that the old foliage can provide protection for the crown during winter,

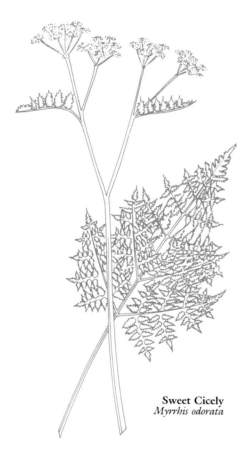

Sweet Cicely
Myrrhis odorata

for it must be remembered that this is a southern European native and a little restless in our climate. Regular cutting back ensures a neat, tidy plant that is well clothed with foliage to ground level, for it is the foliage for which it is grown. The leaves are very finely cut, grey-green, and with a most arresting musky fragrance. Southernwood demands an open sunny position on a well-drained soil, and, apart from being a useful foil for more brightly coloured neighbours, can be clipped into a small formal hedge.

Propagation is by cuttings, the easiest ones to root being of soft, current-season's growth and preferably taken with a heel of old wood. June and July are the best months to propagate, the cuttings being rooted in a standard rooting medium of equal parts by volume sharp sand and peat, or peat and perlite, and offered a little protection. They root within two or three weeks and should then be potted into small pots using John Innes Potting Compost No2. Rather than planting them out during the current year, overwinter them in a frame and plant out the following spring. This is particularly important if you garden on heavy clay. Indeed, it is a wise precaution, when growing southernwood on heavy ground, to have a few rooted cuttings to hand each spring to make good any winter losses. Apart from taking soft summer cuttings, some growers advocate propagation from hardwood cuttings during the dormant period. I have not tried this, but see little merit in the idea, especially as soft summer cuttings are so easy to establish.

SWEET CICELY
Myrrhis odorata *Umbelliferae*

This is a delicate plant with finely divided ferny foliage and spreading umbels of white flowers, loved by bees. Attaining a height of 90cm (3ft), it is a wholesome plant in which every part emits a rich aniseed – celery fragrance. The roots, leaves and seeds have been used for centuries in salads or cooked and eaten. They were alleged to have medicinal qualities that varied widely, from curing stomach ills to acting as a tonic for adolescent girls, as well as serving as an aphrodisiac. The majority of gardeners grow the plant for none of these reasons, its old-world charm and hardy perennial nature being justification enough for accommodating it in their herb patch.

It is an easy-going herb in a sunny position, prospering on all soils with equanimity. It must be raised from seed, however, this being sown in the place where it is to remain, for sweet cicely does not take kindly to being shuffled around. Sow the seed during March and April, eventually thinning the young plants to 30cm (1ft) apart.

TANSY

Tanacetum vulgare *Compositae*

An old-fashioned and well-known herb, which we now grow more for nostalgic reasons than for its decorative, culinary or medicinal value, it once was an essential part of daily life, the strongly aromatic foliage being used to disguise the unpleasantness of tainted food, as a strewing herb, a cure for hysteria and kidney weakness, as well as for preserving human corpses. Nowadays, its only value is to be found in its use as a yellow dye for wool.

Although not an unpleasant-looking plant, neither does it have any great visual merits. A stiff, upright fellow with plain, green, divided leaves and hard, yellow, button-like flowers, it grows in almost any soil in either sun or shade, scrambling about with a vigorous rootstock. It divides readily and can be moved successfully at any time during the autumn and winter. Although no self-respecting herb garden is without tansy, *T.vulgare var.crispum* has much more attractive feathery foliage and is not as invasive as the common kind. Where space is at a premium this is the plant to grow.

TARRAGON

Artemisia dracunculus *Compositae*

This is a plant over which there is endless confusion, both amongst botanists and gardeners. There are in cultivation two tarragons, one of which is referred to as Russian, the other as French. Some botanists separate the two and call Russian tarragon, *Artemisia dracunculoides*, while French tarragon is allegedly *A.dracunculus*. Others consider both to be forms of *A.dracunculus*. From the culinary expert's point of view it is the French kind that is superior, the foliage of the Russian sort being coarse and bitter. To the gardener the main difference is that the French kind will often die out during the winter and, as it does not set seed, has to be increased from cuttings. Russian tarragon, on the other hand, can be raised quickly and easily from seed and seems to be perfectly hardy throughout Britain. Both look similar, with long greyish-green or green leaves, often indented at the ends, and a dense shrubby growth which will reach between 60 and 90cm (2–3ft) high. While the use of tarragon in tarragon vinegar is well known, its leaves are also commonly used in meat dishes, omelettes and fresh, as a garnishing for summer salads.

While tarragon is appreciative of a moisture-retentive soil, it is not happy during the winter in waterlogged conditions. Choose an open sunny site and it will prosper in the mixed herb border, serving as a useful foil for more colourful herbs.

Tarragon
Artemisia dracunculus

French tarragon appears less vigorous than the Russian form and, of course, must be increased by cuttings. These are best taken during spring as vigorous young shoots appear from the crown. Root them in a frame or on the window sill, using a standard rooting medium of equal parts by volume of peat and sharp sand, or peat and perlite. Dip the cut end of each cutting in a rooting compound and ensure that they do not dry out, but equally be careful not to overwater as they damp off easily. When rooted, pot them individually, using John Innes Potting Compost No2. The plants will usually be large enough to plant out by the middle of June. It is not absolutely necessary to root the emerging shoots in the spring, although these produce the finest plants most quickly. Reasonable success can be achieved during the summer by making cuttings of small, soft, lateral shoots. These are best grown on in pots in a similar manner, but overwintered in a cold frame before planting out the following spring.

Russian tarragon is easily seed-raised. Although some gardeners recommend sowing it where it is to grow, most concede that it is better raised in pots and then planted out. Sow in March or April, using any good seed compost. Germination will be rapid and the plants can be pricked out into a tray. There is little to choose between composts, but I favour John Innes Potting Compost No1, the seedlings ultimately being potted on into No2. A spring sowing should produce plants that are ready for putting out towards the end of June.

THYME
Thymus vulgaris Labiatae

This is the thyme to which most gardeners refer, a popular and easily grown subject, much prized for its spicy foliage which is an important ingredient in many dishes. An extract from thyme, called thymol, is the only remaining medicinal virtue, this antiseptic oil being used in gargles and mouth washes. Other medicinal and magic properties such as 'enabling one to see the fairies' have now been discarded! As a garden plant it is superb, especially when given a warm sunny position in a well-drained soil. Under such conditions it will make a tight shrubby, aromatic mound up to 20cm (8in) tall, covered with dense clusters of lilac-pink blossoms that serve as a magnet to bees. Occasionally plants are defoliated in a severe winter. When this happens, cut the damaged growth back to firm wood in spring and allow it to regenerate. By mid-summer the plants will be tight green mounds of foliage again. Foliage can be taken to use fresh or dried at any time up until, and during, flowering. The quality of leaf for culinary use shows a marked deterioration after flowering.

Apart from the ordinary straightforward *Thymus vulgaris*, there are special broad-leafed selections. These have mostly been developed by seedsmen and are grown from seed rather than cuttings, although there is no reason why vegetative means of propagation cannot be employed. In the mixed herb border it is rather nice to include some of the decorative foliage cultivars too. These can equally well be used for culinary purposes, although I think that it is rather a shame to scalp happily growing variegated plants when the more vigorous green-leafed kinds serve just as well. One of the best cream-and-green variegated cultivars is 'Silver Posie' while *T.vulgaris* 'Aureus' is considered to be the most reliable of the golden-leafed kinds.

The fancy cultivars of thyme are increased from cuttings. These can be taken at any time during the summer months, providing that they are of short non-flowering shoots. Any small shoot 2–3cm (¾–1in) long will root readily, especially if detached with a heel of old wood. Use a hormone-rooting preparation in which to dip the cut end and root in an equal parts by volume mixture of peat and sharp sand. Cuttings can be rooted in small pots, pans or trays, but, for the best results, must be afforded the protection of a frame or window sill. As soon as they are rooted they can be potted up into small pots, using any good potting compost, and planted out when large enough to withstand life in the open. The common species and the broad-leafed selections can be raised from seed sown at any time, during spring or early summer, in a good seed compost. As the seed is very fine it is usual to afford a little protection, such as a frame or window sill. Germination is rapid and within a few weeks the seedlings can be pricked out. When large enough to handle, they can be potted up individually.

THYME, LEMON
Thymus citriodorus Labiatae

In most respects this is similar to common thyme, except that it is of a more lax habit, with broader leaves and a very distinctive lemon fragrance. Not quite as resilient as the common kind, this often suffers in severe winters and is not infrequently lost. It is so easy to increase from cuttings, however, that there is no problem in having a young plant or two in reserve in a frame during the winter months in case the worst does happen. If you are really into lemon thyme as a culinary and decorative plant, select the lovely golden-leafed *Thymus citriodorus aureus*. This is multi-purpose and one of the most attractive herbs that I know.

Of course there are a myriad thymes that one could discuss, with endless different scents. In practice it is the common thyme and lemon thyme that are popularly utilised. If you wish to stray off into the diversity offered by these lovely plants, then I suggest the you start with the delicate ground-hugging shepherd's thyme, *T.serpyllum*. Loved by bees for its neat heads of pink blossoms, this little fellow has no culinary value, although in

Thyme
Thymus vulgaris

years gone by it was used medicinally. Nowadays it is a popular flowering plant for growing in the cracks in crazy paving, especially some of the brightly coloured varieties like 'Pink Chintz' and the rich crimson 'Coccineus'. The closely related woolly thyme, *T.lanuginosus*, serves a similar purpose, while the doubtfully hardy, caraway-scented *T.herba-barona* and interesting orange-scented *T.fragrantissimus* are perfect for container- or window-box culture.

VALERIAN
Valeriana officinalis Valerianaceae

This old herbal plant is not the same as the gardeners' valerian, that attractive, but rather rampageous crimson or pink-flowered herbaceous plant *Centranthus ruber*, so often seen at the seaside or on railway embankments. To the herbalist valerian is the much less interesting *Valeriana officinalis*, a tall, rank plant with divided foliage and clusters of pale lilac-pink blossoms with a strange, somewhat sickly, odour. An old medicinal plant, it has no culinary virtues, but is interesting to grow because of its long history in herbal medicine. Any reasonably well-drained soil in an open position will suit it, young plants being quickly and easily raised from seed. As the seeds are not very viable unless fresh, and they also require light to germinate, remember to sow more thickly than necessary and cover only lightly with compost. Seedlings moved into small pots while still tiny establish themselves quite readily, but young plants do not move well unless pot-grown. Therefore many gardeners prefer to sow directly into the open ground during March or April, the resulting plants being eventually thinned to at least 30cm (1ft) apart. This seems quite a wide spacing during the early stages of growth, but is often inadequate later as mature established plants will grow to over 1m (3ft) tall.

VERVAIN
Verbena officinalis Verbenaceae

Another herb with strong traditions, vervain is rarely utilised nowadays. With no culinary value, its claim to fame has been largely mystical and medicinal. It was used in ancient times by the druids and, apart from being a cure for jaundice and dysentery, was also allegedly an aphrodisiac. It has no great decorative merit, but, where space is not at a premium, it should be included in the herb garden. A scrambling and ungainly plant, no more than 45cm (18in) high, it has rough hairy leaves on distinctive, squarish, stiff stems and slender spikes of small lilac-blue flowers. Pretty, rather than beautiful, it is a friendly character to include in the informal border.

Valerian
Valeriana officinalis

Vervain
Verbena officinalis

Although seed can be sown directly where the plants are to grow, much better results are obtained from raising young plants in a decent compost in trays in a frame or on the window sill. Sow the seed during March or April and move the plants on as soon as they are large enough to handle. Box-grown plants can be planted out towards the end of May. Alternatively, short cuttings of non-flowering shoots can be taken during the summer months. These root readily in an equal parts by volume mixture of peat and sharp sand, or peat and perlite, the rooted cuttings then being potted up in small pots in any good potting compost. Once the plants are established in pots they can be planted into their permanent positions.

WINTERGREEN
Gaultheria procumbens Ericaceae

Of all the herbs described here, this is the least amenable to life in a herb garden. While most of the subjects that have been considered benefit from an open sunny position in a well-drained soil, this little North American native is only at home in an acid soil in the shade of trees. An important plant in years gone by for the healing oil extracted from its foliage, this has now been overtaken by modern technology. Nevertheless, it is an interesting, low-growing, shrubby plant with dark glossy leaves, small, white, bell-like flowers and attractive red fruits. It forms a dense carpet of growth and can often be lifted and divided once well established, for it layers itself freely. Short cuttings of the current season's growth can also be taken with a heel of old wood during September or October. Use a rooting compound, dip the cut end of each cutting in this and insert in a mixture of equal parts peat and sharp sand. Unlike the summer soft wood cuttings of many herbs, wintergreen cuttings must be kept cool and are therefore best maintained in a cold frame. They will take until March or April to root properly and then can be potted individually in a good lime-free potting compost.

Woad
Isatis tinctoria

WITCH HAZEL
Hamamelis virginiana Hamamelidaceae

This is not the shrub that most gardeners associate with witch hazel, the popular garden witch hazel being the oriental *Hamamelis mollis*, an attractive winter-flowering shrub with yellow and red spidery flowers. The true witch hazel of the herbalist is *H.virginiana*, an autumn- and winter-flowering species with small butter-yellow flowers on naked branches. Not a plant of great garden merit, it is an interesting subject to include in the herb garden to provide something of a backbone. Its bright green leaves are quite pleasing and turn golden yellow with the first autumn frost. Allegedly growing on any soil with plenty of organic matter incorporated, it is always seen at its best on rich acid mediums.

Witch hazel is difficult to increase from cuttings if you have no special propagation facilities, so it is best to use seed. Imported seed is now available from a number of seedsmen and this should be sown as soon as possible in John Innes Seed Compost. If you sow during late summer, allow the seeds to stand in the open and be frosted during the winter. If, on the other hand, you are sowing in spring, put the sown seeds in the deep freeze for two or three weeks, then bring them out into the warm, when they should germinate. The appearance of seedlings is likely to be erratic and occur over several months. As soon as each seedling is large enough to handle, pot individually in a lime-free soil-based compost. Young plants are usually sufficiently large to be planted out in their second year.

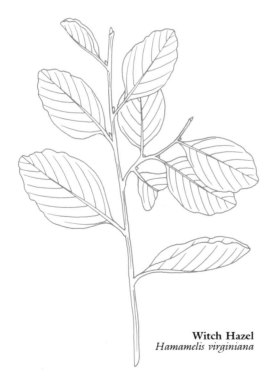

Witch Hazel
Hamamelis virginiana

WOAD

Isatis tinctoria Cruciferae

Not the most inspiring of plants for the herb garden, but one without which no herb garden can be said to be complete. Every school child is taught how the ancient Britons used this plant as a blue body dye long before the Roman invasion. Nowadays it is very much a curio, a strange little plant with rounded glaucous leaves and greenish-yellow flowers during summer, followed by conspicuous dark brownish seeds. Attaining a height of up to 1m (3ft), like many members of the cabbage family it is a biennial, and therefore seed-raised during May and June. Sow where it is to remain, only thinning the emerging seedlings sufficiently to prevent them from crowding one another. A final thinning can be made during the spring when any winter losses can be assessed.

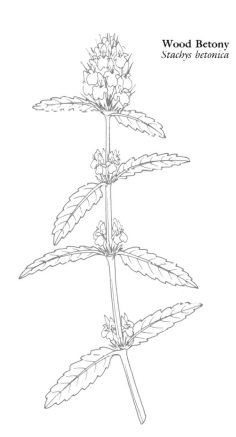

Wood Betony
Stachys betonica

WOOD BETONY

Stachys betonica Labiatae

This is also known as *Betonica officinalis* and is a close relative of the familiar lambs' ears, *Stachys lanata*. Popular in the past for its curative properties, it is now grown more for interest and its historical associations, although some herbalists still brew betony tea, which, if made with fresh leaves, is reputedly intoxicating. Growing up to 45cm (18in) tall, it is an interesting perennial plant with oval, or roughly heart-shaped, leaves and spikes of crimson-mauve lipped flowers during July and August. Although perhaps coarse and vulgar for the formal herb display, it rests at ease in the informal mixed herb border. Short, non-flowering shoots root readily if inserted in a mixture of equal parts by volume peat and sharp sand, or peat and perlite, and are afforded the protection of a cold frame or the kitchen window sill. Rooting is rapid and the young plants can be moved into individual pots in any good potting compost within a couple of weeks and thereafter planted out as soon as they have made a decent rootball. Seed is rarely available, but can be sown in spring, where the plants are to remain.

WOODRUFF

Asperula odorata Rubiaceae

This is a lovely little plant, no more than 20cm (8in) high, with a myriad tiny bright green leaves and starry white flowers during May and June, making it a real charmer for the front of the herb garden where it covers the ground in an emerald carpet. Although a plant of shady places, it seems to prosper in the open on a moisture-retentive soil. No longer used as a herb, either for strewing or medicinal purposes, it is so well loved as to deserve a corner in any herb patch. Seed can be sown during March and April where it is to remain, or the tangled roots lifted, divided and replanted during the dormant season.

WORMWOOD

Artemisia absinthium Compositae

This is an old favourite of mine because of its attractive appearance and ease of cultivation. Indeed, one might say that, given an open situation, wormwood would grow anywhere, seemingly happier in poorer soil. Formerly a herb prized as a cure for intestinal worms, it is now a pleasant foil in the herb garden or mixed border. A roguish plant, it has untidily cut, silvery-grey foliage and insignificant greenish-yellow flowers during July. Spreading by creeping rhizomes, it is easily increased by division during the winter months, although young basal shoots are easily rooted in the same manner as recommended for tarragon.

Appendices

LATIN/ENGLISH INDEX

181

FURTHER READING

BROWNLOW, Margaret   *Herbs and the Fragrant Garden*
Darton, Longman & Todd (1957, 1963)

GRIEVE, Mrs M.   *A Modern Herbal*
Jonathan Cape (1931), Penguin (1976)

GRIGSON, Geoffrey   *A Herbal of All Sorts* (1959)

HEWER, Dorothy   *Practical Herb Growing* (1969)

LOEWENFELD, Claire   *Herb Gardening*
Faber and Faber (1964)

MACLEOD, Dawn   *A Book of Herbs*
Butler & Tanner (1968)

ROHDE, Eleanor Sinclair   *A Garden of Herbs*
Medici Society Limited (1922, 1930)

      The Old English Herbals (1922)
Minerva Press (1974)

      The Scented Garden (1931)
Medici Society (1948)

      Herbs and Herb Gardening (1936)

HARLOW CAR GARDENS

Harlow Car Gardens (Harrogate, North York-shire) are the headquarters of the Northern Horti-cultural Society, a registered educational charity whose function is to provide education and advice for gardeners in the North of the UK. Comprising some 60 acres of landscaped gardens, Harlow Car embraces all facets of home gardening; from vegetables and fruit to annuals, bulbs, herbaceous and alpine plants as well as trees and shrubs. Regular courses and seminars are organised for home gardeners and full-time horticultural stu-dents embark upon their careers at Harlow Car.

The gardens are situated on an exposed site open to moorland winds with a very heavy, acid clay soil. Winter temperatures in recent years have dropped as low as −17°C (1.4°F), but −10°C (14°F) is more usual. Rainfall is 610–710mm (24–28in) per annum, much of which usually falls as snow during the winter. The first frost can occur during early September, while the last one rarely strikes until the end of May. Summer weather is often dry but overcast.

Harlow Car Gardens are situated on the western outskirts of Harrogate off the B6162 Otley road. They are open to the public from 9.00am until 7.30pm or sunset. There is an admission charge for non-members of the Northern Horticultural Society with reductions for parties and senior citizens. Accompanied children are free.

Further details of Harlow Car Gardens or membership of the Northern Horticultural Society are available from The Secretary, Northern Horticultural Society, Harlow Car Gardens, Crag Lane, Harrogate, HG3 1QB.

SUPPLIERS OF SEEDS AND PLANTS

Anglesey Herb Garden

Bryn Golau, Tynygongl, Anglesey, Gwynedd.
Tynygongl (024 874) 2214

Ashfields Herb Nursery

Hinstock, Market Drayton TF9 2NG.
Sambrook (095 279) 392

Chiltern Seeds

Bortree Stile, Ulverston, Cumbria LA12 7PB.

Garlic Farm

58 Churchill Road, Brislington, Avon BS4 3RW.

Glen Haven Gardens

21 Dark Lane, Backwell, Bristol BS19 3NT.
Flax Bourton (027 583) 2700

Green Farm – Cottage Herbs

Thorpe Green, Thorpe Morieux, Bury St. Edmunds.
Cockfield Green (028 482) 723

Herb Farm

Broad Oak Road, Canterbury CT2 0PP.
Canterbury (0227) 52254

Herbs From The Hoo

46 Church Street, Buckden, Huntingdon.
Huntingdon (0480) 810818

The Herb Garden

Thunderbridge, Kirkburton, Nr. Huddersfield HD8 0PX.
Kirkburton (048 483) 2993

Hoar Cross Herb Gardens

Hoar Cross, Burton-on-Trent.
Hoar Cross (028 375) 306

Hullbrook House Herb Farm

Hullbrook Lane, Shamley Green, Nr. Guildford.
Bramley (048 647) 3666

Iden Croft Nurseries

Frittenden Road, Staplehurst TN12 0DH.
Staplehurst (0580) 891432

Lighthorne Herbs

Lighthorne Rough, Moreton Morrell, Warwick.
Moreton Morrell (092 685) 426

Oak Cottage Herb Farm

Nesscliffe, Nr. Shrewsbury, SY4 1DB.
Nesscliffe (074 381) 262

Oland Plants	Sawley Nursery, Risplith, Ripon, North Yorks, HG4 3EW. Sawley (076 586) 622
Old Rectory Herb Garden	Rectory Lane, Ightham, TN15 9AL. Borough Green (0732) 882608
Ryton Gardens, National Centre For Organic Gardening	Ryton-on-Dunsmore, Coventry, CV8 3LG. Coventry (0203) 303517
Suffolk Herbs	Sawyers Farm, Lt. Cornard, Sudbury, Suffolk. Bures (0787) 227247
Tumblers Bottom Herb Farm Ltd.	Tumblers Bottom Kilmersdon, Nr. Radstock Bath BA3 5SY.
Valeswood Herb Farm	Little Ness SY4 2LH. Baschurch (093 95) 376
The Weald Herbary	Park Cottage, Frittenden, Cranbrook TN17 2AU. Frittenden (058 080) 226
Wells and Winter Ltd.	The Street, Mereworth, Maidstone.
Wharton's Nurseries (Harleston) Ltd.	Harleston, Norfolk IP20 9AX.
Yew Tree Herbs	Holt Street, Nonington Dover CT15 4JS. Nonington (0304) 840517

HERB GARDENS TO VISIT

Abbey Dore Court
Herefordshire 0981 240 419

Wheel-shaped herb garden with baytree in centre.

Acorn Bank Garden
Temple Sowerby, Cumbria

The principal National Trust collection, probably the largest herb collection in Britain.

Barnsley House
nr Cirencester, Gloucester 028 574 281

Rosemary Verey's lovely gardens including a formal knot garden and a potager based on William Lawson's *The Countrie Housewife's Garden* (1617).

Cambridge Botanic Garden
Cambridge 0223 350101

Established 1761. Informal herb borders with plants arranged in botanic families.

Chelsea Physic Garden
66 Royal Hospital Road, London SW3
01 352 5646

17th century historic apothecaries' garden with wide gravel and grass paths and formal beds.

Chenies Manor
nr Amersham, Bucks 024 04 2888

Large collection of rare plants in the physic garden; also a medieval well and other historic gardens.

Claverton Manor
Bath, Somerset 0225 60503

The Bath American Museum here houses a small but important herb garden comprising a square layout with beehive at the centre and circular paved path. Herbs grown are those considered essential by the 17th century pilgrims. Also a herb shop.

Cranborne Manor
Cranborne, Wimborne, Dorset 07254 248

Herbs in formal beds, divided by grass paths and leading to a central sundial; also a knot garden.

Edinburgh Botanic Gardens
Inverleith Road, Edinburgh 031 552 7171

Established 1670: culinary medicinal and poisonous plants on display.

Eyehorne Manor
Hollingbourne, Kent 062 780 514

15th century manor house with gardens in the process of being restored. Includes an informal profusion of herbs and old fashioned plants such as roses, violets and Roman chamomile.

Fulham Palace
Hammersmith, London SW6 01 736 7181

Restored knot garden edged with clipped box.

Gaulden Manor
Tolland, nr Taunton, Somerset 09847 213

Traditional cross shaped herb garden with brick paths and central sundial. Interesting comfrey hedge.

Glasgow Botanic Gardens
Great Western Road, Glasgow 0141 334 2422

Traditional herb garden in ornamental layout with turf paths.

Hall's Croft
Old Town, Stratford upon Avon, 0789 204016

Tudor style garden created in the 1930's. Elizabethan medical dispensary worth seeing in the house.

Hatfield House
Hertfordshire 07072 6872

Jacobean house with a large herb garden and central sundial. Chamomile seats and an interesting collection of herbs. Also an open knot garden featuring 17th and 18th century plants.

Kew Gardens
Kew, Richmond, Surrey 01 940 1171

Fine parterre created in the 1950s to a traditional design. Also a sunken 17th century garden and good example of chamomile seat edged with box.

Knebworth House
Knebworth, Herts 0438 812661

Tudor House with herb garden based on a series of circles and designed by Gertrude Jekyll.

Knole
Sevenoaks, Kent 0732 53006

Traditional style 'wheel' herb garden where the spokes are made up of silver, gold and green leaved plants. Made for Lady Sackville in the 1960s.

Leeds Castle
Maidstone, Kent 0622 65400

Culpeper herb garden and fine historic castle.

Little Moreton Hall
Congleton, Cheshire 02602 2018

Lovely half timbered moated manor house with knot garden and Elizabethan herbs.

Lytes Cary Manor
Ilchester, Somerset

National Trust property once the home of the Lyte family – Sir Henry Lyte wrote the *Niewe Herball* in 1578 and made a physic garden at the manor. Today you can see herbs that would have been familiar to Sir Henry.

Michelham Priory
Upper Dicker, Hailsham, East Sussex
0323 844244

Tudor house with 12th century origins and reconstruction of a monastic garden. All plants were grown in England in the 16th century and divided into groups according to the disease they were believed to cure eg: herbs for digestion.

Moseley Old Hall
Wolverhampton 0902 782808

Faithful reconstruction of a 17th century knot garden based on a design laid out by Rev Walter Stonehouse in 1640.

Museum of Garden History
St Mary at Lambeth, London SE1 01 373 4030

Adjoining the churchyard where the Tradescants are buried, gardens include a knot garden designed by Lady Salisbury. All plants were known or discovered by the Tradescants.

Oxford Botanic Garden
Rose Lane, Oxford 0865 242

Established 1621 making it the oldest physic garden in Great Britain. Plants laid out in classification beds.

Oxburgh Hall
nr Swaffham, Norfolk 036 621 258

Elizabethan moated manor house with interesting elaborate parterre filled with cotton lavender.

Sissinghurst
nr Cranbrook, Kent 0580 712850

Vita Sackville West's lovely gardens (now National Trust). Informal herb garden loosely based on the cross shape and surrounded by a yew hedge. Read *Vita's Other World* by Jane Brown (Viking) before you go.

Large chamomile lawn.

Springhill
Moneymore, Co Londonderry, N Ireland
064 874 48210

12th century monastery herb garden reconstructed from the old Anglo Saxon lists.

St Michaels Mount
Penzance, Cornwall 0736 710507

Tudor Museum
St Michael's Square, Southampton 0703 24216

Knot garden taken from *The Gardener's Labyrinth* by Didymus Montaine (16th century) edged with dwarf box and cotton lavender. Other interesting Tudor garden features.

Wisley Gardens
Ripley, Woking, Surrey (0483) 224234

RHS collection.

Index